Kaleidoscope:
A Collection of Poetry

By
Chenise Lytrelle

Kaleidoscope: A Collection of Poetry
First Edition
Copyright © 2008 by Chenise Lytrelle

Anointed Publishing Company
A Division of Lytrelle & Company
HYPERLINK "http://www.anointedpublishingcompany.org"
www.anointedpublishingcompany.org

Photos of the author and cover design by Kieshalia Stephens
© Pink Afterglow Photography

Photo of May Lois Bright McCray used with permission.

Printed in the United States of America

ISBN 978-0-615-25069-4
Library of Congress Cataloging-in-Publication Data
2008908433

The following poems are reprinted from
Life's Lessons © 1996 by Chenise Lytrelle

Life's Lessons
The African-American Mother
Just People
The Chosen Ones
I Love Summertime
Passing the Torch
My Heroine
Making A Difference in this World
Hope for Tomorrow
A Self Love
Mommie's Order

In Loving Memory of
My Mother-in-law

May Lois Bright McCray
Sept. 15, 1945 - March 7, 2008

Contents

Chapter 1
Love & Happiness

Chapter 2
Bruised, But Not Broken

Chapter 3
In God We Trust

I Prayed For You
Just A Prayer Away
Turn Around
Redemption
Only God Can
A Work In Progress
My Soul Cries Out
The Miracle
I See God In You
You Must Understand
You Will Know
Sunday Meeting
Stand Strong!
Faith

Chapter 4
In Honor of Those Who Came Before Us

The Inaugural Poet
The African-American Mother
Reaching Back
We Are African-American Women
Woman Of God
Don't You Dare
My Heroine
Determination
Christian Women Warriors
For Those Who Came Before Us
Passing The Torch
History Makers
A.M.E. History

Chapter 5
Fountain of Youth

I Love Summertime
The Giggle Box
Back In The Day
The Circus
Poetry
Life's Lessons
Cousins

Chapter 6
Unto Everything There Is Season

Students & Teachers
Indescribable
Miscarriage
Cancer
Likeness
Chocolate
Just People
This World
In Spite of Myself
This Mess-age
Self Description
Stolen Innocence
Barack Obama
Our Place
Making A Difference in this World
You Are
Baby Boy
Unbroken
The Chosen Ones
If I Had Known My Father Well

Chapter 7
The Ties That Bind

Kaleidoscope
Hope for Tomorrow
Grandfathers
Grandmothers
Mothers
Family
Tribute To Mom
Sisters-In-Law
My Granddaddy
A Connection Of The Heart
My Sistergirls
Motherfriends
Friendship
Good Men

Chapter 8
Celebration of Life

Until We Meet Again
We Will Not Forget
You Are Missed
Divine Intervention
The Daughter Of A King
Freedom's Price
The Last Goodbye
Mistaken Identity

Chapter 9
Tributes to the life
of
May Lois Bright McCray

Ode to Granny
Still We Praise God
Don't Forget How Much I Love You
Time
Storm
Auntie's Poem
Ready or Not
Losing Someone

Chapter 10
New Voices

Why?
Questions I Ponder
We Are Strong
I Love My Mom
Poem 1
Poem 2
Poem 3
Inapt
Inspirable Person
Prayer Is The Language Of God
My Mother Is Like
The Duality Of Love
Balance
Lies
God's Sacred Covenant
Our Generation

Love and Happiness

Our Babies

(For Imani Jovan Williams and Isaac Malik Williams)

You have brought
Into our lives
A joy that is hard to express,
Simple to comprehend and
Complicated to speak of.

Your smile has brightened
Our days and turned our clouds
Into pure sunshine.

Your kisses have put
A new meaning into
Our vocabulary for
Ways of expressing love.

Your face, just moments after
You were born
And perhaps even before,
Is etched in our hearts.

Your voice rings in our ears
Even when we are not
In your presence.
It sings the song of
Happiness, joy,
Innocence and love.

Your life has
Made us mature
In ways we had reserved
For years to come.

For now,
We are praying for the strength
To guide you,
To teach you;
The way that
God would have us to.
He has entrusted you to us
And we intend
To fully comply
With His guidelines and direction.

The Ultimate Joy

When I first saw you
The tears that welled up in my eyes
Gave way to the path down my cheeks,
And there I felt the warmth
Of my tears on my face,
The same warmth that I felt
Within my heart.
Never before has there been such a
Feeling of love and joy,
And never again did I feel
This overwhelming happiness…
Until again I gave birth.
In every way I experienced
The complete goodness of God
And His mercy as it shone
On your face,
In my heart,
And in my arms,
As I held you after your
Grand entrance into the world,
And it was then that
I felt the ultimate joy.

True Love Never Dies

(Written in honor of and recited at the 50th Wedding Anniversary of Ruby Farrington & the late William Farrington)

True love grows
With each minute,
Each hour,
Each day.

It is like a flower
Which blossoms brightly
In Spring.
And as the conditions
Of the seasons change,
The condition of true love,
Does not; it stays the same.
True love withstandeth all things.

It symbolizes peace,
As does the presence of a
Pure white dove.

It is patient and understanding
Through trials
And through strife.
True love is triumphant,
For its existence is eternal—
It faileth not!

True love surpasseth
All things,
For it is truly
A gift from God above.
True love never dies!

Recalling When...

I am looking for something definite
That would direct me as to
Why I love you from the depths of my heart.

I am looking for something permanent,
Perhaps a big sign that would
Tell me why you mean the world to me.

I am searching for the message
On the answering machine
That led me to this fallen state of
Confessed loyalty.

I am pondering the moment
That I knew that you were
The one for me.

I am sketching the
Photograph of you that
I carry with me at
All times in my mind.

I am looking for the signal
That told me to go forth
With my obvious
Attraction and devotion.

I am trying to remember
The first time that
I realized how much
I truly loved you.

Sometimes

Sometimes all I want
Is for you to hold me
In your arms and
Tell me that everything
Is going to be okay.
But we get so caught up into our success
That we seldom share time that way.

Sometimes I want to say
Let's just take a walk today,
But the hours seem so short and
The office always calls late.

Sometimes I want to sit and look
At the children play in the park,
But our meetings keep us out
Late into the evening
And when we finally get home,
It's dark.

Sometimes I want to take a vacation,
Just you and me,
But the kids come home from college
And we have to take them shopping.

Sometimes I can't remember
What it was like being a family.
But nowadays we're business partners and
We only talk over lunch.

Sometimes I want to give you a kiss,
But there are always too many people around
And we wind up shaking hands
And nodding to one another.

Sometimes I want to just be Mrs.
Rather than the Chief Executive Officer
And since some of my sometimes
Seem like possibilities,
I respectfully resign.

If Life Were Different

If life had dealt us
A different hand,
You and I may not be here together.

If life had dealt us a different span,
Our days might have been much shorter.

If life had taken a different turn,
Ill-fated or in great favor,
You and I might not have known
How good we are
For one another.

If life had blown
Me through the winds
On yet another sail,
The course might not have taken
Me to you, my darling love.

If one of those days
We spent together had not turned
Into what we know as tomorrow,
We might not have known
That we were each other's destiny.

If God had not been so gracious
As to bless us with the gift of one another,
We might not have ever known
The depths of our commitment—
The plan that only God knew...
Our love.

Submission

I wanted to cry…
But anger wouldn't let me.

I wanted to scream…
But my hurt clamped my trembling jaws shut.

I wanted to say some things
To hurt you the way
That you had hurt me…
But when I tried to speak,
The words escaped me.

I wanted to be angry
With you from now until…
But God suppressed it immediately.

I wanted so much to hate you,
But the love I have for you
Overshadowed it…
And I decided to give in.

From This Day Forward

On the day that you exchanged
Vows before God,
You pledged to share
Each minute, each hour, each day,
Each year and all of those to come,
Together and with total devotion.

But interruptions occurred
Along the way and
Before either of you realized it,
Time had not been your friend,
For you had not used
It wisely and had not
Kept those vows,
Not wholly and completely,
And most times not even
Partially.

And so you tried again
To alter your bond
To strengthen and compress it
Into something significant,
And days, weeks and months
Went by before you moved
Into the direction
Of togetherness,
And once again you were
Separated.
Separated by outside interference,
intrusion and confusion,
You were parted by untruths, fabrications,
Infidelity, assumptions and misunderstandings.
Broken apart by inward pain
From outward trials and sins
And failures and guilt
And unresolved issues

Of molestation, rape, separation,
Divorce, adultery, favoritism,
Bastardism, misplaced priorities,
Emotional abuse, physical abuse
and perceived neglect,
And insecurities and other indignities
Of your broken childhoods.

And then in the midst of
Counseling sessions and prayer vigils
And maturity—
Both yours and his—
You came to know
That the madness of your lives
From minor to extreme
Must stop at this point and go no further,
So as not to be passed on
To your children
So that instead of brokenness,
They will see wholeness
And instead of its evil twin
They will know, identify and mimic
Fidelity,
Protection,
Compassion,
Trust,
Devotion,
Hope,
Spiritual substance,
Kept promises,
And know without a shadow of a doubt
What it means to be
LOVED!

Admission

You became a man
Right before my eyes—
In the moment that you uttered
The words "I'm sorry."

You gave me a new perspective
From which to look at you now,
As soon as you revealed your thoughts,
Taking full responsibility for your actions
And justifying nothing,
Yet searching for a way to move forward
Without the weight of this pain.

You showed me a side of you
That I recall vividly falling in love with
And it is a memory that I hold dear to me—
Even in this state of confusion.

Your words erased my
Heavy burden and comforted me
And brought me a peace that I'd forgotten could be,
Just by saying
"I'm sorry."

A Love Story

*(Written in honor of and recited at the
50th Wedding Anniversary of James & Virginia Wilson)*

From the smallest of third grade eyes
To the opinions of young instrumentalists,
You have changed lives
In ways you may never know.

More than 50 years ago,
The union that took place between you
Was God's ordination for love.
When you met in the seventh grade
You had no idea that even then
He was molding you into greatness,
Perhaps in those young years
You didn't know
That love would be the outcome.
But today, in reflection, it could have only
Been the work of the Good Master.

The compassion of your hearts has
Been seen through the lives you have lived
As teachers, community workers, church members,
And most of all, friends.
You have influenced those
That have passed through your classrooms,
Your homes, your churches,
That may never return
To say their thanks,
But to others they tell
"The Wilsons are wonderful people."
When God blessed your union
With Jamia and Jamiel,
He was allowing you to create more models
Of goodness, of kindness, of strength.
And over the years,

As you added to your parental number
Through the surrogate children you have taught,
You passed on the same tradition that you
Had given to your daughters.
What a blessing it was for them to share you
With all of Eccleston Elementary and
Jones High School—
Adding to their siblings,
1,000's more.

When I was in the third grade,
One of you taught me that being smart is a gift,
And in high school, the other taught me
That it was okay to be smart.
You taught me that learning music required knowledge,
Skill and studying,
And that there was no easy way out of learning.

You have no idea what influence you have had in my life,
As well as in the lives of countless others.
From one of you I learned patience,
Humility, and understanding.
From the other I learned to stay ahead of the game by
Studying, not just my music,
But my "lesson" as well.
Admittedly, I didn't always put your
Lessons into practice, but Chief, you know
That you always taught us that
"Practice doesn't make perfect,
Perfect practice makes perfect."
Now, almost 25 years after knowing you,
I find that I am instilling these values
Into my own children as well as

The children that I now teach,
And others whom
You have taught,
Are doing the same things.
You are the forefather and foremother
Of generations of excellence,
Created through your unselfishness,
Through your endurance,
Through your hard work,
Through and because of your dedication
To young people and to mankind.

Your rewards here on earth have been many,
But perhaps the one that will count the most
Will be the love that is given to you now,
So that you will know that your work
Has indeed been effective,
That your kindness and love
Have transformed lives,
Attitudes and thoughts,
That will be carried on
For generations to come.

For every life you have touched,
For every wound you have bandaged,
For every hand you have held,
For every tear you have dried,
For every paddle you have given,
You have created a family of people,
Who now are parents,
And grandparents themselves,
Who are better because of it.
You deserve every flower that you receive,
Every accolade that can be written or read,
For you are the love story that sparked
Generations of excellence.

A Selfish Love

Give me your heart,
Let me consume
Its every part
With joy and
Continuous laughter.

Give me your mind,
Let me incapacitate
Your thoughts with
The joy that my mere being
Has already brought you.

Give me your hand
Let me exhume
The power and warmth
Of my love.
In all of its full beauty
And splendor
By squeezing it tightly,
Completely and passionately.

Give me all of you,
For I am equipped
With the gift only
To love you fully,
Just as you are.
In my own selfishness
I require more than
Just a fraction of
Your love.

A Love Like This

I know it sounds crazy,
But he'll always be my baby.

I know it sounds strange,
But this kind of love will never change.

I know you think it's sad,
But I can't even be mad
At the man who
Loves me enough to
Help me fulfill
My wildest dreams.

I know you thought
We'd thrown in the keys
To the field of love,
But we have only begun
To unlock the entrance.

I know that you
Don't understand this
Connection,
And unless you know
A love like this,
You never will.

Lost In You

(For Abayomi)

In your arms

I am lost.

I can be found only by

Your gentle release —

I love it when you hold me.

In your presence

I am confident

That there is protection —

I love it when you reassure me.

In your heart

I am carried

And I receive your love

In action, deed and thought —

I love the way you love me.

I Wait For You

I wait for you
With bated breath
To love me.

I wait for you
With outstretched hands in the night
To come to me.

I wait for you
To pick up where we last left off
To bring jovial smiles to your face.

I wait for you
To see me just as I am
With all of my imperfections meaning nothing.

I wait for you
To know that you are my one true love.
Oh, how I love you
Until the end of time.

I wait for you
To love me the way that
My heart beckons,
Begs, screams, longs…
To be loved.

I wait for you
To love me.

His Love From A Distance

He taught her that her unfairness
May be a result of her own fears,
But she is sometimes unfair anyway.

He has shown her that she can
Release her fears without
Picking them back up
And returning them to their original state,
But she is still afraid not to be fearful.

He has demonstrated a concern
For her that she thought would have
Elapsed after the initial entertainment
That her plight seemed to bring,
But she was proven wrong by his
Continual love for her.

He has displayed an influential
Side of himself
That he is unsure of possessing
Because he wears his past hurt like a cloak
And it covers his beauty,
Just as it covers hers.

Yet he tries to show his beauty to her
As it peers through
Every word he speaks,
But she is so frightened that fear
Controls her responses to him,
And she is unsure if he is trying
To teach her, love her, control her,
Manipulate her, embrace her or push her away.

Non-Responsive

Your words have comforted me
On many bleak occasions,
But as I reach out
To embrace you,
You are non-responsive.

You have sent encouragement
In my direction,
Given me words that
Uplift and empower me,
But as I reach out in gratitude,
You are non-responsive.

You show your fondness
By checking the status
Of my life, my being, my health,
But when I reach out to acknowledge
Your concern for me,
You are non-responsive.

You celebrate,
Though from a distance
Every triumph and achievement
That I make,
But when I reach out
To include you in my excitement,
You are non-responsive.

Feelings

I feel rejected
As I tenderly touch you
And find my hand
Removed, pushed away
With the rumbling voice
That says "goodnight."

I feel dejected when
I reach out to touch you
Only to find that you
Have moved in another direction
To avoid contact with me.
And you joke about having
No "pda" (public display of affection),
Though we've been together
For many years.

I feel vacated when you
Entertain your friends
In our home,
But never want to go
When I'm visiting mine.
You keep it separate,
Presenting it as equal,
But I know it's another
Way for you to be
Cruel to me over time.

I feel forsaken when you
Don't encourage me to
Let my wings take flight.
It's as if I gave up my dreams
And you kept on fulfilling
Yours, in spite
Of what we had

Before us.
But I held on because
I believed that you'd
Eventually realize
That I am the
Love of your life.

Mommie's Orders

I saw him today
Underneath my
Window,
Traveling swiftly
As though he were
Running from something
That frightened him.

In my heart
I knew that the
Right thing to do
Was to
Stop him,
Grab him,
Kiss him,
Love him,
But I am confined
To the concrete walls
That surround my
Upstairs room,
For my mother
Has forbidden me to
Fall in love.

You

You have brought new meaning

To the words "I Love You."

You have shown me

Through your actions that

Together we can conquer anything.

You made me see

That life is as much about love

As it is about laughter.

You have given me

A new reason to smile

Even in the midst of adversity.

You have taught me

That the only way to overcome

Is to believe in the power of love.

Deployment

I wondered if the time
Would make us understand
Or if the days that pass would
Simply span the distance between us,
Or never change a thing.

I wondered if the days
Would help to ease the pain
Of our separation
And if it would
Help us to see the errors of our
Deeds and ways toward each other
When we reach a stumbling block
Or a hurdle.

I wondered if something would
Magically shine, showing us the light
That tells us that neither of us
Is always totally right or wrong or perfect.

I wondered if we'd learn
That at the end of the day,
We should always come to an agreement.

I wondered if we'd ever find
The pieces of our heart that
People say seems to sometime evaporate
As time progressed and
We were forced apart
By military obligation.

I wondered if despite the
Extended length of time,
If God would be merciful enough to
Bring it all to an end

And maintain the love and kindness
That had been our foundation.

I wondered if the interference
We'd endured from this removal
Of our physical union
Would cause some irreparable harm.

I wondered if you were
Going to be returned home to us safely,
With your body, spirit and mind
In tact, as they were upon your departure.

And then I wondered,
As I lay dreaming in the night,
And I was awakened to
Remember that you were home from the war
And that I was lying safely in your arms.

Childhood Friends

(For Joe & Trudy Edwards)

The beauty of a
Brown-skinned girl
Innocent, beautiful, bright
Waiting for the bus to
Go to school
Where she meets a young boy
Brown-skinned and handsome
Smart too.

She looks around and
Seems to find
A boy who is ordinary,
But still he is special.

Taught her a lesson
On tic-tac-toe
Spanked her a few times
'Til she got the
Hang of the game
And shamed him
When she won.

Friendship sets in
And days keep
Starting and ending
Before you know it
They've grown up
To become
A woman and man.

Time passes and then…
They fall in love.

Missing You

My pillow is wet

With repeated tears as I

Think of the years

We've spent as one…

      Love can be so cruel sometimes.

Falling on my knees

Praying to God for relief

Remembering your kiss…

      Love can be so painful sometimes.

Going through the day

Wishing you were here

To hold, to love, to feel..

      Love can be so comforting sometimes.

Trying to carry on

In your absence from my world,

Needing to feel you near me…

      Love can be so hopeful sometimes.

Bruised, But Not Broken

Protection

I cannot release my heart to you,

Not completely,

For each time I relinquish

A portion of it,

You give it back to me,

Shattered and broken

On a silver platter

Decorated with the parsley of falsified

Love and honesty.

Instead of love,

You fracture every piece,

Abusing it without

Regret or concern.

For the balance of time

I will engulf this beating

Part of me,

Somewhat still alive

Trying to keep each piece intact

So that you can never tear it apart…

Again.

Do Not Register

I am elated to

Know that I rated high enough

On your meter,

To register as worthy to

Be loved by you

But since the years

Have proven to me

That your love

Does not bend,

Does not comfort,

Does not support,

Does not protect,

I would prefer

That my existence

Not register at all.

Restoring Order

For years now
We've been a team
Cheered and slam dunked
With great joy and pride
At the achievements
We've made over time.

We've seen our share
Of ups and downs
In life and in the world
As we know it.

Though things have changed
And life's been hard,
We each have gained
Our own honor for the cause.
But somewhere along the way
We've lost our focus,
Taken our minds
Off of what's important.
We've placed things above people,
And put God to the side,
And we have the audacity to wonder why
The gap between us is so wide.

Perhaps we'll redirect
Our interests and place order
Where it is due,
Accepting our proper roles,
Instead of me trying to be you.

Survival

in a place of quiet rest

i find the inability to pass the test

to linger where my heart doth lie

and find in time a deeply muffled sigh

that tells me i am doomed

and life will always carry gloom

in time i'll know if i can be

someone other than me

i struggle to be

a productive part of society

my mind wanders and at times

i am lost

in dreams and thoughts

i think i'll survive this thing called "life"

if ever i can hear the voice

that tells me to keep on in spite

of everything i have been through

Life

from birth we

experience our first

pain as the doctor

hits us on the bottom

to provoke our first cry…

and we spend the rest of our lives

being hit by the

blows of life from every angle…

and we continue to be provoked,

and we continue to

shed tears

Mask

refusing to trust

hiding behind

the mask that

covers the essence

of who you are

missing some small

link to your heart

depriving yourself

of a chance at

happiness

Unexpected Change

without probable cause

you withdrew

stopped being the person I knew

took away the joy

you'd originally given to me

because based on what I'd seen

i had already become wrapped up in you

Release

Your love for me
At times chokes the
Life out of me
It causes me to
Regurgitate on the
Things I held dear…
I need to be released.

Your love is blinding
When I'm trying to see
What's ahead of me,
It incapacitates my foresight
And causes me to be unsure…
I need to be released.

Your love causes
Me to hyperventilate
And I loose track
Of the direction
In which I thought
I was destined to travel…
I need to be released.

Heart Attack

from the depths of my soul

it calls from deep beneath

the surface of my true self

it hollers and howls

hoops and screams

until it seems

there is no outlet for me

i toss and turn

to untangle the

knife in my heart

but it is wedged

beneath the top layer

producing a myocardial infarction

from the aches and pains

of betrayal

Unspoken

shattered and scattered

broken, bruised and beaten

black and blue

inside and out

in all places in between

the scars that cannot be seen

the ones within my heart

Meaningless

Repetitious sounds

That whisper "I'm sorry,"

After the 100th time

You did the same ole' thing again

And repeated those same meaningless words

Like you were

An automated machine.

A Blinded Eye

I saw the handwriting on the wall

But I turned my head and pretended

That everything was fine.

I felt the knife in my heart

But I grabbed my chest and

Stood up tall as though I

Hadn't been wounded at all.

I sensed the distance you were placing

Between us,

But I tried to hold on to you

Despite the fact that your actions proved

That you were incapable of truly being able

To love me.

Retaliation

sinful thoughts of

hurting you

the same way that you hurt me

drive me into a shell

that closes off the world

that hides my pain

to cover me like a mask

hidden by my smile

I need the truth to rescue me.

Fragments

fragile pieces

fragments, like broken glass

sharp, penetrable, keen

left from my

attempt to love you

and expecting to

be loved in return

tortured hope

diminished capacity

ended vision

closed case

never to be reopened

Immeasurable

Give me the kind of love
That comes without preparation.

Give me the kind of love
That has no need to be
The basis of fear and regret.

Give me the kind of love
That leaps walls,
Stretches the span of time
And finds no boundaries.

Give me the kind of love
That is patient,
Kind,
Gentle,
Secure,
Confident,
Selfless,
And protective.

Give me the kind of love
That is faithful, unquestionable,
Honest and sincere.

Give me the kind of love
That is bold and daring,
The kind that is so abundant that there
Is no way that it can be measured.

Searching

love without measure

unrequited affection

lonely in a crowd

searching for confirmation

begging for affection

longing to be loved

Unintentional Lessons

He did it to you,
Took away your belief in
What was right and what was good
The moment that you saw him
Beat your mama,
Wish you could've jumped in the fight,
But it was never your battle.

He did it to you,
Made you think that
The only way you could be a man
Was to speak with your fists
And you didn't know how
To tell her you loved her,
Unless you beat her every day.

He taught you to never
Stand up and take responsibility
For your own actions,
To never look yourself in the eye or
Take responsibility for yourself
And your numerous insecurities.

He taught you that,
Probably because he learned
It from his father too.
And when you decide to
Really make a change,
A change from the heart,
You might leave this jail cell
A changed man,
A real man,
One who uses his voice to express his needs,
Instead of his fists.

Betrayed

the wound was unexpected
caught me by surprise
came from a place unseen
shared with you my life's journey
spared no detail
when I spilled my pain
thought you cared about
the progress I had made
but you kept me from
communicating with you
my trust you had claimed
reached out for you at the height
of a difficult time
made yourself unavailable, intentionally
contact, at your discretion
in the shadows I realized
that you were a friend of convenience
yours and yours alone
concerned, when you wanted to be
maybe even non-existent
couldn't fool myself anymore
realized that you'd been
entertained by my plight
thought we were bonded
but the connection was on my end
thought you'd be there for me
in the seasons to come
my heart had already warned me
just before I'd reached out for your ghost
told me I'd be better off
by myself, void
the way you left me
in my time of need

One Sided

The first time I saw you

I was immediately smitten

Your touch intoxicated me

And your words assured me

I knew you were the one

The moment our eyes met

I fell for your slickness

Maybe it was your smile

Or the lies that you made

So very real and true

I fell in love with the fantasy

That you'd painted for me and you

Misunderstood the games

Took me a long time to realize

That I was in love

All by myself

Farewell

Farewell to envy

It has no place here

Farewell to jealousy

It's already caused enough division

Farewell to hate

It has been the core of much sadness

Farewell to deception

It has blinded many innocent

Farewell to hope

It devoured reality

Farewell to daydreams

They take the focus off of what is real

Dreams

Keep your dreams before you
Implant them in your heart
Envision yourself coasting
High above the clouds
Forget about what you were told
Was impossible to achieve
Forget about the ones who didn't believe
In you and in your dreams
Don't allow the past to cloud
The direction that you are going now
Soar beyond your imagination
Command your concentration
To reach the edges of your desire
Reach out your hand
Touch it!
The sky offers no limits
Go beyond its heights
And depths
Push through
And rise
To become a new you
Wipe the bruises away
Keep on climbing the mountain
Find its peak
And fly on the wings of an eagle

In God We Trust

I Prayed for You

I prayed for you
When every opportunity
Presented itself.
I asked God to keep you
In His loving care…
Because I could not.

I prayed for you
Whenever the thought arose,
And God knows that I prayed
From the bottom of my heart.
I asked Him to keep you
Steadfast and strong.
I asked Him to keep you
Away from danger and harm.

I prayed for you on days
When I felt that things weren't right.
I asked for insight
Into your heart
And power to understand
Your rights and wrongs.

I prayed for you and
Heaven knows I was sincere,
But I must confess I prayed
For you sometimes
Through many tears.
I prayed for you on holidays
And all days in between.
I asked God for many things,
But mainly to return you safely to me.
I prayed for you when things were rough.

They got so bad sometimes
I could hardly remember when they were smooth.
And I asked the Lord
To bless us both,
You and me,
Through and through.

I prayed for you
And I still do,
Not just because I think I should
Or just because it's right.
I pray for you, my sweetness,
With all my love and might.

I pray for you at every thought
And I don't intend to quit,
Because my prayers are being answered,
One at a time,
Bit by bit.

Just A Prayer Away

When it hurts too badly
To put into words,
When no audible communication
Will form from your mouth—
 God is just a bent knee away.

When it keeps you up all night
Tossing and turning
In your sleep—
God is just a whisper away.

When it occupies your thoughts
And hinders your daily progress,
As a mother, a father, a sister, a brother,
A friend or other loved one—
God is just a closed eye away.

When the pain embeds itself
In the crown of your heart,
In the tears of your eyes
And the tongue in your mouth,
Call on Him!
He's just a prayer away.

Turn Around

You possess what many see in you,
But you do not even know
That God has given it to you.

You glow like the stars in the night,
But you can not see it for the
Darkness that covers your eyes.

It has been prophesied that you
Have angels on your shoulders,
But you close your ears when
They try to speak to you.

God is waiting to
Come into your heart,
But you keep it closed
Because you allow
The devil to hold it prisoner.

There is so much good
For you to do in this world,
But you will never know
If you do not redirect
Your energy.

Tomorrow is not promised to you,
But it surely can be given,
If you will just
Turn your life around.

Redemption

It's been a while now
And it is abundantly clear
That yesterday will not return and
Tomorrow is not promised to you.

I know the hours seem to come
Just as you anticipated that they would,
But have you ever considered
Who gave you the air to breathe?

You see there are always three sides
To every thing.
In fact there are really three:
That's the way I see it
The way you see it,
And then the actual facts.

God has given us the choice,
And the road map is the key.
He says to come to Him in need
And he will set you free.

He promises that what He says,
Is nothing more than true
And that His way is the entry
Into the gates for you.
There is no doubt about it,
If you try Him you will know,
That the preciousness of God
Is the only way to go.

He will nestle you
In His bosom,
Caress you with His care,
Speak with power
In your ear
And make all your
Thoughts aware.

It is the God of Abraham,
Jacob and Isaac too
Who creates the life
Of every man
Regardless of his Hue.

For more than words
Can express,
More than a tongue
Can confess,
Right at the request of anyone
Is the invitation for
God's eternal life
And His amazing grace.

Only God Can

My heart is full of deep remorse
For thoughts of hurting you.
My prayer is that I can
Give my hurt to God
While allowing Him to
Work it through.

In times of sorrow and of pain—
During the weight of the storm and the rain
When the prayers are difficult
To pray
And the tears just won't go away,
When sadness overshadows fear
And doubt enters both far and near,
When trials consume
And pain resumes,
When hurt confines and deceit invades,
I know that it's only God that
Can take the hurt away.

A Work In Progress

I am searching for the one thing
That will ensure me
That my transformation is complete.
Perhaps a sign from God to tell me
That I have run the race
And that I've "arrived,"
Just the way He wants me to.

Despite the occasional slip of the tongue
That says a word that is succeeded by
"Oh excuse me,"
And my attempt to treat all people with respect,
And amid the timid reaction of those who
Ask me about my Jesus transformation
Lead me to believe that I have
A long way to go.
Perhaps I am what one would call
A work in progress.

My Soul Cries Out

My soul cries out with

Somber sounds of pain and

Grief and sorrow and a hint of joy.

It is filled with the songs of

Years gone by that were

Full of anticipation and

Disappointment and new beginnings —

With good and bad endings

And hopes and dreams

And so much it seems

That the days behind me

Are sometimes as painful

As the ones in front.

But still I step

With pride and ambition,

With prayer and hope

That someday there will be

A balance for my soul,

And when I cry out to the Lord

That with great certainty,

I will be able to

Release it to Him completely.

The Miracle

The time has finally come.
It is upon you, right now
And in this moment
You are on the
Brink of a miracle and…
You don't even know it.

You have always possessed the power
To change,
To transform,
To overcome,
To conquer,
To grow,
To expand,
To heal.

The miracle of God has
Already stared you in your face.
It looked back at you.
It is your reflection in the mirror.
The spirit of God has entered you.
It is the difference in the way
That you see people and things.
The power has been given to you.
Now, you have to be willing
To let the miracle take place
In you.
You possessed the miracle
All along, and didn't even know it!

I See God In You

(For Charlene Stallworth Allen, Jeanette Collier, Willie McDaniel Coller, Jolene Ezell, Sandra Forsythe, Eugenia F. Forté, Minnie Harris, Mary Henson, Charmaine Jenkins, Loretta Jones, Jessie Newman, Precious Robinson, Geneane Pearson, Berry Steward, Crystal B. Taylor, Jill Trier, Juanita Collier Verreen, Al´Maria Williams and Brenda Williams)

I see God in you.
The light shines
So brightly and clearly
That I am almost blinded,
Yet I am comforted.

The beauty of God
Radiates through you,
And the greatness of God
Is manifested in your stare.

I see God in you—
In your walk,
In your life,
In your being.
When you speak softly or with fervor,
I hear God in your words.

I feel God in your hugs,
For your embrace is one
Void of judgment and full of love.
I know God through your eyes,
And I am secure in your company.

For your love and kinship
Is the presence of God.

You Must Understand

I realize that I can be difficult at times—
That I can be impossible to get along with,
But you must understand that
I come to you with a thousand footprints
On my back.

I realize that
It is difficult for you to understand
My constant state of protectiveness,
My failure to release my feelings
And my withdrawal from the world,
But you must understand that I am
Attempting to protect myself
Against hurt, harm and danger.
You see, I have been trampled on
For a very long time.

I realize that you are trying to
Convince me to be open and
To open up freely to you,
But you must understand that
My heart has been closed for a long time.

I realize that you are only trying
To make things better for me,
But you must understand that the
Wounds are much deeper
Than just my broken flesh—
They are engrained in my heart
They incapacitate my thoughts.
They control my fear.
They hinder my progress.

They choke my words…
And while I want to,
Need to,
Pray to,
Hope to,
Finally have the opportunity to be free,
I am wounded by slavery
And its atrocity is in me.
So please keep me in your prayers
As I try my very best
To get used to this thing called freedom,
And try to forget my master's whip.
For the days ahead are blurry
Though the past has been so clear.
I asked God to help me reach here
And now I feel confused,
But just like those who came before us,
I, too, can find the courage
To stand strong and proud.
For in just a matter of time
I know that God will give me the strength
To enjoy the beauty of freedom,
Liberty and victory.

You Will Know

(For Rev. Dr. Arlene Churn)

You will know that
God is deeply embedded in her heart…
The moment you hear her preach.

You will see the
Glory of God…
The moment you hear her preach.

You can feel the anointed
Presence of God…
The moment you hear her preach.

You will be drawn to
His word through her delivery,
Unaltered, undoctored, uncorrupted, unpretentious…
The moment you hear her preach.

You will embrace
The will of God for your life
And His divine plan…
The moment you hear her preach.

You will understand
The vivaciousness of living
A life for Christ…
The moment you hear her preach.

You will feel the touch of God
And His presence will surround you…
The moment you hear her preach.

You will know
It's Him when she stands,

You will know that they are His words
Through her,
As she dawns the pulpit,
You will know that the
Message is especially for you…
The moment you hear her preach,
You will know.

Sunday Meeting

Sunday meeting comes
Dressing up ain't fun
When you've got to put
On all those clothes just
For a few hours.
Stockings, hair ribbons,
Old ladies smelling
Like lily perfume
Pinch your jaw and say
"How cute!"

Squeeze you so hard,
You forget to breathe
And you pray that
Your pressed hair
Doesn't go back if
It gets hot and you
Start sweatin'.

Sliding down in the seat
When Mama catches the
Holy Ghost 'cause you
Shame of her hollerin'
And jumping around
And carryin' on.

Preacher finally talks
His hoop and holler
Gets the crowd going
And then he opens
Up the doors of the church.

And all you
Can think about is
Your stomach growlin'
And that fried chicken
That Mama has waiting
For you at home.
It's a great day
When Sunday meeting ends!

Stand Strong!

(Inspired by my aunt, Ethel "Jean" Sinclair)

Stand strong
In the knowledge
That God is the keeper
Of your soul
The comforter of your journey
Called "life".

Stand Strong
During the trial
Even though you may
Go through the fire
It's only a test
Of your true faith.

Stand strong
Knowing that your
Belief is the substance
Of your strength
The corridor of your
Walk of faith.

Stand strong
In the peace
That only God can give to you
This gift is non-transferable.

Stand strong
For the generation
That came before you
Stand through their
Triumph, struggle, victory,
and their tears.
Stand Strong!

Faith

Your faith is the
Only way that you
Can overcome adversity,
Without it you are exposed.

Your faith is the
Key to unlock the
Power that lies within you,
Without it you are powerless.

Your faith is the
Premise to your boldness,
Without it you are hidden behind
The victory within.

Your faith is the
Essence of your superiority,
Without it you are mediocre.

Your faith is the
Imprint to your survival,
Without it you would fail.

Your faith is the
Culmination of your goodness,
Without it your deeds are meaningless.

In Honor of Those Who Came Before Us

The Inaugural Poet

(For Dr. Maya Angelou)

She stood at the podium
In the graceful presence
That only her 6 foot frame can give
Commanding the attention of her audience
By rolling her shoulders back,
And then,
In her rumbling voice
She spoke.

And she moved the rock,
And the river,
And the tree and she spoke
To the hope of young girls
And young boys
As she rattled words that meant
We were ready for a new beginning
And a new tomorrow
And a new love for our
Fellowman and our neighbors.

And she peeked into
The morning's eyes
And reminded us of
"One nation under God",
And for a moment in history,
People forgot her gender,
And put aside her race,
And judged not,
For her words gave way
To the heart of the matter,
And we were filled with
The fresh dew of
Unity and democracy.

The African-American Mother

My color is specifically
A definition of my strength.
My eyes display the
Character that I
Possess inside.

My personality contributes
Largely to my graceful style.
My spirit is a symbol
Of my longevity.
My lips are a sign
Of my charm.

My love is an attribute
Of my African-American heritage.
I am the keeper of the dream,
I am the reign of the family,
I am the African-American mother.

Reaching Back

Respect, Kudos and Homage
To extraordinary women
Who are reaching back
As they climb forward,
Who dance to the beat
Of a different drum,
Who lift the sounds of the
Motherland from their lips,
Listen to the women…
They carry Africa in their words.
They sing songs from their hearts.
They are mothers and grandmothers.
They are aunts and sisters.
They are daughters—
Learning from their elders,
Hearing of the struggle from
Those who know best.
This is for the women
On the brink of their mothers
And grandmothers and great grandmothers'
Dreams
Of being able to
Do anything and everything.

Kudos to great African-American women
who bring forth liberty.
From their mouths
Escape words of courage
And of encouragement—
Words of homage and praise.
They sing the songs of
Freedom and advancement.
The words ring like the sound
Of civil rights marchers'

Chants and hymns
With arms interlocked
Marching,
Marching,
Marching
Into freedom land.

This is for the women who
Reach back as they climb forward,
Bringing forth the hopes
Of a young girl,
The promise of a young boy,
The hope of a generation—
Completely oblivious to the sacrifices
That were made
To pave the way
For who they are,
Who they can be,
Who they wish to be,
During this day and time.

We Are African-American Women

We walk with the grace of Diahann Carroll,
Move with the rhythm like Debbie Allen and
Speak with the passion of Eleanor Holmes Norton.
We mesmerize with the candor of Dorothy Dandridge
And heal hearts like Oprah Winfrey and Andrea Sullivan.
We are activist like Marian Wright Edelman.
We are generations of excellence
From Harriet Tubman to Condeleezza Rice,
And Ain't We Women, like Sojourner Truth?
We strut like Eartha Kitt,
Write like Nikki Giovanni and rhyme like Nikki Grimes.
We lead and follow in the footsteps
Of Shirley Franklin and Dr. Dorothy Height.
We possess the presidential character of Shirley Chisolm,
Dr. Trudie Kibbe Reed, Dr. Johnetta Cole
And Dr. Juliane Malveaux.
We shimmy like Josephine Baker,
Katherine Dunham and Judith Jamison.
We are the diversity of African-American women.

We have the audacity of Angela Davis,
The down-to-earthness of Phylicia Rashad,
The ageless charisma of Cicely Tyson,
And the elegance of Camille Cosby.
We carry the torch of Jackie Joyner-Kersee
And pass the baton like Gail Devers,
Michelle Finn-Burrell and Marion Jones.

We swing the racket like Althea Gibson
And bring new flame to the court like
Venus and Serena Williams.
See us in a new form as we dunk the ball!
Watch Lisa Leslie and Sheryl Swoopes
On or off the court

There is no shame in our game.
We own sports teams like Sheila Johnson.
We are the agility of African-American women.

We weep for the loss of Coretta Scott King
Remembering her contributions to continue "The Dream."
And we stand in ovation of the legacy
Orchestrated by Myrlie Evers-Williams.
We lead organizations that promote and
Uplift our people like Sandra Miller Jones.
We are the progression of African-American women.

We sing like Billie Holiday,
Our blues are in every tune.
We relax to the music of
Roberta Flack and Sara Vaughn.
We hit high notes like Patti LaBelle.
We produce like Tracey Edmonds and Suzanne dePasse.
We are actresses like Angela Bassett,
Lynn Whitfield, S. Epatha Merkerson,
Jada Pinkett Smith and Sanaa Lathan.
You may never know what role we are playing.
We educate like Marva Collins.
We are university professors and scholars ourselves,
Like Dr. Barbara Cotton, Dr. Vivian Hobbs, Dr. Margie Rauls,
Dr. Beverly Guy-Sheftall and Dr. Leesther Thomas.
We are advocates and catalyst for young people like
Mona Humphries Bailey, Dr. Cecilia Griffin Golden,
Carol Brunson Day and Jaleesa Hazzard.
We explore the literature of our people like Dr. Eleanor W. Traylor
And still we rise like Dr. Maya Angelou.

We have the range of Jesse Norman
And the scat of Ella Fitzgerald.
Leontyne Price is our poster girl.

We've inherited the legacies of Dorothy West,
Barbara Jordan and Esther Rolle.
We preserve the stories of Toni Morrison,
Valada Flewellyn and Jackie Torrence.
We are the memoirs of Gwendolyn Brooks
And Zora Neale Hurston.
We live the words of best selling women writers.
As author Rosalyn McMillan wrote,
We're "One Better" than the rest.
We are the courage of African-American women.

We are the scribal contributions of
Bebe Moore Campbell, Alice Walker, Tananarive Due,
Anita Bunkley, Tina McElroy Ansa and J. California Cooper.
We are the "Women of Brewster Place"—
Our place is everywhere and anywhere we choose.
As author Debrena Jackson Gandy encouraged,
We are searching for all the joy we can stand.
We are the works of Gloria Naylor,
Nella Larsen and Daryl Dance.
Our destinations are as unknown
As Mae Jameson's astronauting
And our futures will be captured
On the films of Julia Dash.
We are as "Young, Gifted and Black"
As Lorraine Hansberry foresaw.
Yes, we are every woman.

We are affiliated with women's organizations
Like Alpha Kappa Alpha Sorority, Inc,
Delta Sigma Theta Sorority, Inc.,
Sigma Gamma Rho Sorority, Inc.,
Zeta Phi Beta Sorority, Inc.,
The National Council of Negro Women,
And community and professional organizations
Of many kinds.
And some of us are not affiliated,

Yet our commitments to work within
And for the community is abundant!
In the grand scheme of things,
We are all united,
By the sisterhood of life!

We are the "Quiet Strength" of Rosa Parks.
We are the empowering strength beside presidential
Candidates like Michelle Obama.
We edit like Susan Taylor, Janet Hill,
Gayle King and Marcia Gillespie.
We preach like Dr. Arlene H. Churn, Cathy Hall-Johnson,
Bishop Vashti McKenzie and Renita Weems.
We inspire like bell hooks.
We are entrepreneurs like Madame CJ Walker.
We make comebacks like Tina Turner.
We reflect the beauty of Halle Berry
And the advice of counselors like
Julia Boyd and Dr. Linda Colbert.
We bring to life the work of
Ntzoke Shange and Pearl Cleage.
We direct like Valencia Matthews and Vinette Carroll.
Our jobs are never done.
We have the appeal of Jasmine Guy
And the versatility of Audra McDonald.
We are *Sweet Honey in the Rock.*
Our sights and sounds are sensational.

We aren't "Waiting to Exhale" —
We're preparing to inhale
The blessings of life and womanhood.
We are ready to receive the
Divine opportunities that our foremothers
Have given us;
Ready to breathe life into
Yet another generation of excellence.

Our connections are born through
The kindness of love and
Nurtured through the breast of understanding.
We are aunts and nieces,
Mothers, daughters and cousins,
Mentors, sisters and friends.
We are African-American Women.

Woman of God

When God decided to make woman,
He decided to do so with
A special touch,
A special design,
A special plan,
A special purpose.

When God decided to make woman,
He pulled out all the stops.
He sat on His great throne and
Peered down from Heaven and said,
"I am ready to make a new woman,"
And He breathed the breath of life
Into your mother's womb
And soon,
After God's abundant protection,
Your parents became the proud
Recipients of the life of this
Beautiful brown baby girl.

And they named you,
Giving you something that
The world would always use
To know who you are and whose you are—
Their beautiful brown bundle of joy!

God knew that one day
You would rise up to be
Called a blessed woman for Him!
He knew that one day
You would venture out
Into this brutal world
And be a warrior
On His battle field,
And He knew that your sword
Would be His Holy word.

Even in the Word,
He tells us that He knew you
In your mother's womb,
Which explains that your
Very existence is His handiwork
And in your life,
You must live the life,
The abundant life,
That He has prepared for you.

In your life,
Women speak of you in high regard.
They honor the gift that your life
Has been to them
And to those around you.

They know that you are a
Born-again believer—
On-fire-for-the-Lord woman,
A teaching and preaching woman,
A child of God,
A walking angel of God,
And most of all, a lover of God!
There is no need to tread lightly
Or to tread in fear,
For God's protection was
With you from the beginning,
And it remains present and clear.
Don't fret and don't be afraid,
For every promise that He made
Is still the same.

Be strong in your stand,
Courageous in your walk,
Bold and phenomenal in your being,
For you are a blessed
Woman of God!

Don't You Dare

Don't you dare question her calling,
Remaining in the past
When women weren't allowed
To breathe, to walk or to live
Without a man's permission.

Don't you dare
Inquire about whether or not
God called "her,"
Just because you believe that He
Could have called only "him."

Don't you dare
Disrespect the woman of God
By refusing to honor
Her calling,
Refusing to invite her to the pulpit,
Refusing to address her by her
Holy title,
Don't you dare!

When God created woman,
He gave her no boundaries
Under which she could serve Him,
And the woman of God
Who stands tall in the pulpit,
Who kneels as she enters the throne of grace,
Whose robed glory stands to preach the word,
Is ordained through the Master,
And she shall be honored.

Don't you dare try to slight her,
For you will find that,
Her calling is so powerful,

Her presence is so dignified,
Her message is so anointed,
Her words are so elevating,
That she brings to
The ministry
A perspective
That no man
Could see,
For he has not walked
A mile in her shoes.

She was the woman
With the issue of blood,
And she was Martha and Mary,
Trying to find that good part.
She was a prophetess and a preacher
And a pastor and a leader
And she will,
With or without your acceptance,
Continue to bring the Word.

My Heroine

(For Dr. Maya Angelou)

She walks with
The grace of God.
Her voice rivets
With power and
With prestige.

Born into this world
As Marguerite—
Destined to become
The best!

Through struggles,
Strife, misery,
And through pain,
Odds stacked against her—
She has made the
World a new one.

Making monumental
Strides that can
Never go unnoticed,
Shining through each
Poem that she creates
And recites.

The epitome of womanhood—
That is what she displays.
An integrity
Never before
Known to man,
A demeanor
Of love, peace
And pride.
Full of victory

Towards overcoming
Life's trials.

Unabashedly, she
Represents our people.
Not just African-Americans,
But all people,
For selfishness holds
No place in her heart.

Through her works,
An attempt to efface
All racism, sexism and superiority
Is made.

She has no need
To display ostentatiously
The talents that God
Has so graciously given her,
For her gift flows
From every line
Of her poetry and
Gives delight to
All who embrace her literary work.

With fortitude and dignity,
She discusses the
Heritage of many,
Tracking back to our
Ancestors' triumphs,
Finding the one thing
That connects all races,
The one thing that we
All have in common:
Love!

With grand illumination,
Character, pride and might and
Confirming belief in all of us—

She writes.

To all mankind—
No one in particular,
For her writings focus
Towards no boundaries—
A lost soul,
A troubled spirit,
A battered mother,
An abused child,
The hopeless,
The homeless,
The bereaved,
The spirit filled—
There is no limit
To those she has reached.

For no matter what
The color of our skin
May be, our hearts
Are all the same.
This is her pledge,
Her message,
Her intent.

The essence of
Humanitarianism,
A role model for
All mankind,
Clever, witty,
And intelligent,
In a category
All her own.
A cultivating spirit,
A fluent tongue,
Outstanding vitality
In a peaceful disposition—

She leaves a literary
Legacy to us.

The woman, the poet, the educator,
The enthusiastic sister,
A lover of all mankind—
My heroine,
Dr. Maya Angelou.

Determination

Come my brothers and sisters,
Gather at my feet.
Listen to the sound of my voice in
This melodic tone.
My voice is heard in every key,
And I am not ashamed to speak my mind.

I have been a victim of circumstances,
But from them I have gained knowledge and wisdom.
I am a woman fully,
And wholly,
Without fail and without doubt,
Through and through.

There is nothing that
I am afraid to face,
For I believe that
I can conquer anything.

I helped to build pyramids long years ago,
I gave birth amidst the cotton in the fields,
And kept right on working,
Never missing a beat—
Without regard for myself,
For I conjured up whatever
Strength was needed.

There is no obstacle
Too large for me to tackle,
For my strength is
Not measured in weight
Or in wealth,
And not even in deeds,
But it is measured by
The size of my heart
And the size of my
Determination.

Christian Women Warriors

*(For Debra G. Allen, Susie Brown, Rebecca Spencer Butler, Gwen B. Baker,
Shirley Carson, Dr. Linda Colbert, Laura B. Ellis, Mary Counts Frazier,
Joyce Henry, Ophelia Bright Hines, Augustine Hoze, Dephrin B. Jackson,
Annie R. Johnson, Connie Jones, Ruthie Kleckley, Patricia Lovell, Barbara
Mullings, Susie Myers, Mary Bright Palmer, Altamese Pinder, Hazel Rodmon,
Sylvia Stallworth, Dr. Clara Walters, Eartherlean Williams and Ceddie Wilson)*

We are a great breed of people,
We women.
We are the vessel through which life erupts —
The womb through which creation evolves
And the heart through which love
Is first conceived.
We are a great breed of people —
We women.

From the rib of Adam to the garden of Eden,
We are the preparers of yesterday's dream,
Tomorrow's promise, and today's hope.
We are a great breed of people —
We women.

We come in many forms —
Mothers, sisters, aunts, grandmothers, friends,
Missionaries, preachers, first ladies, church mothers,
Deaconesses, members of the usher board,
The auxiliaries, the nurses' guild.
We give what has been given to us
To the generations in transition
To educate and enrich —
Hoping they will emulate
What it means to be
A woman,
A God-fearing woman,
A woman of God,
A church-going woman,

A faith-filled woman.
We are a great breed of people—
We women.

Our gifts are not unwrapped in one
Location or on one specific thing,
We are a multitude of talents under the tree—
Servicing every need,
Mending every broken heart,
Advising wives how to love their husbands,
Telling them to be chasten and faithful
And to be good mothers and sisters and aunts
And friends to other Christian women.
We are a great breed of people—
We women.

We preach and teach,
Pray and say,
That God is the way
And through Him
Our womanhood is never in question.
We care not if a woman has
Given birth through labor pains,
As we know that anyone is
Capable of mothering,
From the heart,
From what God naturally gave her.
We are a great breed of people—
We women.

For Those Who Came Before Us

For those who have come before us,
Who have endured storms
During the raging waters of life
From the slave ship
To the cotton fields
To the segregated lunch counters
From coast to coast
In search of the same
"Freedom and justice for all,"
We have been empowered by your victory.

For those whose strength prepared the way,
Whose perseverance and courage was the foundation
For each of us
To thrive
To stand
To flourish
To endure
To achieve
To triumph
To soar
To heights unknown,
With unlimited possibilities.

From cosmetics to opera,
From literature to athletics,
From education to congress,
From sculpting to civil rights,
From music to politics,
From medicine to law,
From the Harlem Renaissance to contemporary fiction,
From prose to poetry,
From anthropology to theology,
From media moguls to Tony Award winning actresses,

From law to order,
From slavery to freedom,
We honor you—
We honor your endurance,
We honor your gifts,
We honor your contributions,
We honor your presence and imprint in this world,
For you are
African-American women
Who came before us
And your lives,
Your treasures,
Your blood, sweat and tears,
Are why we can
Move toward a better tomorrow.

Passing the Torch

(In honor of Mona Humphries Bailey)

I am a woman:
Black, brown, beige,
Yellow, red, tan, coffee—
Powerful in my presence,
Serious in my tone,
Stately in my stand,
Erudite in my conversation,
Scholarly in my presentation,
Confident in my being—
I am a strong black woman.

As meek as the day is long,
As soft as cotton and as smooth as silk,
As dainty as a rose—
I am a beautiful and delicate black woman.

Don't take my long strides lightly,
I mean business about my causes,
I'm an advocate for education,
I'm a spokesperson for success.
My life is symbolic of dynamic triumphs,
For I have overcome insurmountable odds—
I am an open book,
You may read me if you please—
I'm a mighty black woman.
Take notes, if you will—
You can learn a thing or two.
I'm a competitive, articulate,
Well-dressed, well-prepared,
Well-informed, well-aware,
And a very appropriate
Example of womanhood—

Epitome describes me best.
Excuse me if I seem
To toot my horn,
But I have seen and endured
Battles of segregation, integration,
Depressions and uprisings
For civic, social and gender rights.
I have survived and will continue
To strive for the empowerment
And advancement of my people—
I am an enduring and confident black woman.

Magnificent in my achievement,
Phenomenal in my excellence,
Superb in my existence—
I am a powerful black woman.

Honor and respect my victory,
Embrace my courage,
Catch my contagious spirit,
Spread my love, support my causes—
Together we will continue
To conquer and to grow.

Allow yourself to be empowered,
Empower someone else,
Be an honorable black woman,
Pass the torch onto someone you love!
We are historic black women.
We are wonderful black women.

History Makers

*(For Orlando History Makers; Mable Butler, Dr. Olivia Allen
Chaney, Carolyn Fennell and Annetta Wilson)*

History makers

Historic role breakers

Women of phenomenal achievement

Tasks to be completed

Skills that cannot be duplicated or repeated

Originators of change

Variation and range

Progress for our people

Recognition for womanhood

Breaking the glass ceiling

Over and over again

History makers

Historic role breakers

Continually defying odds

Excellence in its entirety

Purposes, plural

Accomplishments for all

Beauty and success

Scholarly and educated

History makers

Historic role breakers

A.M.E. History

*(In honor of Bishop Vashti McKenzie, the first female Bishop
of the African Methodist Episcopal Church)*

Through the grace of God

She journeyed to a sacred place

Between the walls of

Change, opportunity and faith

Placing herself amid

A role only held by

The male gender

But God spoke,

And gently He touched

The hearts of the people

And with the democracy

Of America and of the church,

They placed her at

The helm of leadership

Making history

Showing their faith

In God and in her God-given ability…

And she became the first to be called

"Bishop."

And time stood still

As this appointment took place

As she stood between the walls of

Change, opportunity and faith.

Fountain of Youth

I Love Summertime

I love summertime
'Cause you can drink
Lemonade and kool-aid.
I love summertime
'Cause you get sandwiches
For lunch and you
Don't even have to sit
At the table.
I love summertime!

I love summertime
'Cause your parents
Forget the hour of the day,
And you stay outside late in
The evenings,
Playing,
And don't even really know
How late it is.
I love summertime!

I love summertime
'Cause my yellow skin
Turns golden, reddish brown,
It's gorgeous! And
When I remove my watch,
I am two different shades of brown.
I love summertime!

I love summertime
'Cause I gain weight from eating junk food
All day long,
And my grandfather calls me round.
I love summertime!

I love summertime
'Cause you can dance all day
And have lots of fun,
Nobody cares if you walk or run,
And you can eat ice cream
Two or three times a day.
I love summertime!

The Giggle Box

(For my little giggle boxes; Gregory (II) & Kennedy Baker, Bianca & Giana Fiore, Nicole Goldberg, Le'Maya & Omari Johnson, Sara Khan, Stefan Lupu, Collin Saunders, Gisel Suarez, Mark & Richard Volynski and Alexander Wang)

The laughter started
And would not end.
It could not, would not, did not end.
It started on the right side of the room
And spilled and spilled to the middle,
And just when we thought that the
Laughter was over,
We giggled some more and started
A giggle explosion.

Oh, we laughed and we cried
And we tried and tried
To make it stop,
But the giggle box
Would not, could not, did not stop—
It just moved like a germ
From person to person
And kept going and going
Until we all felt the motion.

And we laughed and we laughed
And we laughed some more,
And then our giggle box
Threw us on to the floor.
Oh what fun we had as we
Held our stomach and wiped our eyes
'Cause we laughed so hard that
We started to cry.

And finally we felt the giggle go down
And we calmly picked ourselves
Up off of the floor
Until one of the kids
Started to giggle some more.

Oh we laughed and we laughed
and we laughed some more,
'Cause we knew that soon the principal
Would come through the door
'Cause we were having
more fun than allowed,
and our schoolmates probably thought
we were getting too loud.

But we could not, would not,
Did not stop until we ran out
Of things to laugh about!

Back In The Day

(For Birto (Sr.) & Joanne Benjamin)

Do you remember
Back in the day
When you'd get in trouble
At school,
And before you went home
Down that dirt road,
Mama and Daddy
Already knew what you'd done?
We were such a community
Back in the day.

Do you remember that
You'd be better off to tell the truth
Because the lie you told
Would cause you to get a whippin'
Far worse than
You could ever imagine?
We were so obedient
Back in the day.

Do you remember playing
Outside with your friends
And racing down the street
To make it home
When you saw that the street light
Was about to come on?
We were so trained
Back in the day.

Do you remember when
Everyone looked out
For everyone,
And people sitting on

Their porches weren't scared
To speak, or to look
Or even to be seen,
Because we spoke each time
We saw each other,
With a wave and a greeting?
We were all family
Back in the day.

Do you remember when
Liking someone was
As simple as checking
The box for yes or no
To declare your affection?
We were so sweet
Back in the day.

Do you remember when
Love meant holding hands
And kissing meant
You were promised to
Each other?
We were so appropriate
Back in the day.

Do you remember when
Using fowl language
In the presence of an
Adult was a sin,
Punishable by a belt strap?
We held ourselves to standards
Back in the day.

Do you remember
Waking up early for Sunday School
And going to the store to
Get a piece of gum,
Before somebody could catch you?
We were so innocent
Back in the day.

Do you remember
That the best thing
About getting up to clean the house
On Saturday morning,
Was finishing up early
So that you could go outside to
Play hopscotch, Little Sally Walker,
Jacks, Miss Mary Mack, jump rope
And double dutch?
We were so creative
Back in the day.

Do you remember
The look your mama or grandma gave
You while you were in the choir stand
Chewing gum or playing with your friend
And they were on the pew or
Standing up ushering,
And you knew that it meant
You'd better cease and desist
Your foolishness right then and there?
We were so understanding
Back in the day.

Do you remember when
Sunday dinner was when we all
Gathered around the table
And spoke words of thanks to God
Before anyone lifted a finger to eat?
We were so faithful back in the day.

Do you think that
Maybe a part of our problem today
Is that we've forgotten
Our yesterdays,
Trying to get tomorrows
That stole our values
And the core of who we were?
We were so connected
Back in the day.

The Circus

smiling faces

eyes stretched in amusement

children laughing

enamored by the action

mesmerized by the

tricks and the unicycle

the flying trapeze

the clowns making noise

elephants standing

tigers jumping through hoops

ringmasters in control

memories created for a lifetime

Poetry

Poetry moves me,
Shakes me,
Makes me
Feel like
Everything is going to be alright.

Poetry lifts me,
Takes me,
Up and away
To a place that gives me comfort and joy.

Poetry fills me,
Thrills me,
Like the greatest excitements of life.

Poetry consoles me,
Controls me,
Demands that
I honor the rhythm within.

Poetry grooves me,
Soothes me,
Like a
Hot bubble bath after a long winter day.

Poetry inspires me,
Conspires with me,
To tell
The stories that are in my heart.

Life's Lessons

*(For my godmother and first grade teacher,
Jean "Patricia" Hurley Wilkins)*

When I was a little girl
Swinging from the trees
With my beautiful Sunday dress
And church shoes on,
You always made me get down
And you brushed me off.

When I refused to do
My homework because
I thought that it was unfair,
You never gave me an option.

When I was out of hand and
Chose not to be a nice little girl,
You smacked my hand and
Demanded that I behave.

When my mouth became too flip
And language a bit foul,
You put soap in my mouth
And made me write hundreds
Of sentences on the board.

When I sassed adults,
You made me apologize
And never once asked me
If I meant it or wanted to.

When my smile was large
And my heart was full
And I was content,
You implored me to enjoy it.

When I was sad and crying uncontrollably,
You dried my tears calmingly,
And assured me that
I should learn from them.

When I wanted to give up
On life,
You never gave up on me.
You just continued to remind
Me that I was fully equipped
To handle anything,
For you had taught me
Life's lessons.

Cousins

(For Shalunda Alderman, Tressa Cummings, Vinetta Frazier, Sheila Hill-White, Yalunda Johnson, Jermaine Johnson, Shantrell Johnson, Ceyretta Jones, Danyell Gates-Little, Felicia Nix, Rodney Nix, Mario Nix, Patrick Nix, Jovanni Sanders; In Loving Memory of Duwan Maurice Johnson)

Playin' in the park

Swinging high on the swing

Like a diving board into 12 feet

Not a care in the world

No worries, not a thing

The monkey bars called our names

Wearing dresses, what a shame!

Dirt in our shoes

Ponytails swinging from side to side

Jumpin' rope, takin' turns

Little cousins, middle cousins go first

Big cousins take their turn last,

Gotta oversee the younger crew

Make sure they understand what to do

You'll be held accountable

When granddaddy, auntie or uncle ask

What happened?

Street races to the end of the street,

We all know which ones of us always gets beat

Big cousins combing little cousins' hair

Decorating it with bows too pretty to play in

That ain't fair!

Tryin' to keep us cute and clean

But we wanted to go outside
Not stay in to play board games,
Like Hungry Hippo and Monopoly
Granddaddy said "Hush that fuss!"
When we got too loud
Auntie said we could stay up late
But Sunday school was the morning date
No exceptions, no excuses
We weren't under the delusion
That there was a choice involved in church
All the cousins gathered,
Older ones, young ones and the ones in between,
House to house,
Place to place,
One big happy family tree
The best memories of our childhoods
Together we were a team

Unto Everything There Is A Season

Students & Teachers

They appear before you,

Eagerly sitting in concert—

Waiting for it.

Thirsting to be quenched

With raised hands

And bright eyes,

They are the receivers;

You are the giver—

Together there is

Learning!

Indescribable

(For Jean Bryant)

If I had to put
Into exact words
Exactly how I feel about your kindness…
I would be speechless.

If I had to write down
How much you mean to me…
The pages would be filled to capacity.

If I had to show
You how precious I think you are…
I wouldn't know what emotion to display.

If I had to give instructions on how
To compute the calculation of your worth…
I would be unable to figure an absolute number.

If I had to program your goodness…
The computer would not have enough memory space.

If I had to describe the attributes
About you that make you so special…
I would still be making a list
Until the end of time!

Miscarriage

We wandered today
Past the forbidden area of the store,
Though we'd promised ourselves
That we'd bury our pain
By forgetting everything.

But before we were aware
We were looking at
Pacifiers, diapers and cribs—
Searching for the unknown answer
To console us through this struggle.
And as we ran our fingers across the bedding,
We realized that this cruelty,
Maybe a punishment from God,
Was not one that we could ever understand.

So much hurt and so much pain,
And time had not been a healing force
And love couldn't overshadow our pain,
And still we were in the midst…

The laughter we thought we'd share,
Watching our baby boy or girl
Smiling and playing
Was void in our ear,
And in our hearts were the memories
Of the thoughts we'd hoped to share—
Wishing we could have touched a hand,
Or felt the breath on our cheek,
Or even had the chance to clean up
Spit up from our clothes.
When we hold on to this thought,
We hope to capture just a glance,
But the memory quickly fades

For it is just a daydream.
And the sadness incapacitates our heart,
And we embrace
To find some consolation for a time
There is so much pain,
And so much hurt
And time has not been a healing force
And we are still in the midst...

Cancer

(For those brave enough to fight for survival)

slipped up on me

like an old parking ticket

came back to haunt me

like a bad decision.

took away my confidence (and my hair)

replaced it with disdain

had me so angry and confused

i couldn't remember my name

took away my joy

gave me agony and pain

made me regurgitate

things haven't been the same

thought I sent you packing

but you came back again

extended to a greater margin within…

my life you tried to claim

still I pray that

there will be grace

when God decides to

heal my body

and I'll send you packing

on your way to the graveyard

to be buried—

instead of me

Likeness

There is a likeness in all of us
That shows through the windows
Of the soul.
We smile and laugh,
But the somber spirit in our eyes
Tells the tale of our lives.

It tells the tale of
Happiness and joy.
It reflects the sorrow
Of our past and sometimes
The very present.

We see through this likeness
How much we really are the same,
Although we often want to believe
That we have nothing in common.

We are branched together
By the tree of life.
Its leaves, some gingerly moving
Entities, light and heavy
In autumn colors of
Red, orange and brown
And in the fragrance of summer green.

Chocolate

sometimes in the midnight hour

when I am overwhelmed

or early in the morning

when I need a lift

when I take up the notion

to need a little something more

to bring me to peak

to a point where I perform my best

when I think my best

i am consoled by one thing...

chocolate!

Just People

When I sit and stare out of my window,
I see many things that are appealing
To my eyes.

I see children playing,
People laughing
And joy flowing from afar.

But sometimes when I look,
Things are not as I think
America should be.
In my eyes,
I do not always see freedom,
Nor do I see liberty.

I try not to see things in black
Or in white
Nor in dark or in light,
But how can I see things fairly
In a land that is
Bound instead of free?

I pray that one day this nation
Will be united,
Not divided.
That my children may
Be allowed to see the world
Made up of just people —
Like you and like me.

This World

This world has
A certain way of
Making you folks think
That it owns you,
That you could not
Possibly pave your own way
Or create your own destiny.

In this world
You fall prey
To the set boundaries
That at times
Chokes the life
Out of dreamers.

In this world
Sometimes a parameter
Is set in such a way
That it
Stifles creativeness
Shuts down uniqueness
And ends dreams.

This world says
That you have to be a certain way,
Dance to a specific beat,
Earn a certain amount,
And live in a particular community.

But defying the standards of this world,
Standing up and making
A new path,
Taking a new direction,
Setting out to do

That which others
Said cannot be done…
That's how you show this world
That there are no rules,
No boundaries
No parameters
No specifics
And there is still room for dreamers.

In Spite of Myself

I see a beauty in you
That I cannot describe.
It is a part of why you
Are so very dear to me,
Perhaps it comes from
The gentle way in which
You sometimes carry yourself,
Or the calm tone in
Which you give your
Opinions on matters—
Both great and small.

You always seem to know
Just how to inspire me,
And you enlighten me
By sharing bits and pieces
Of your protected self.

I am afraid at times
To let my pure self free
And divulge to you
The true essence of who I am—
The bruised, but not broken
Side of me that sometimes
Separates me from
Reaching my full potential.

But I am refreshed by your honesty
And your subtle presentation
And example
Of the way that you believe
Life should be—
Peaceful, quiet, uninterrupted,
Private, unassuming, secluded
And reserved.

I am better because you've added
Your perspective to my view,
And I am eternally grateful
That despite my flaws,
You seem to embrace me anyway.

A Message for This Mess-age

We cannot give in
To the world's
Definition of us.
We cannot succumb
To the low standards
That have been set for us.
We cannot prove
True the cadence
That has been played
Mocking our intelligence
And questioning our integrity.
We cannot permit ourselves to give in
To the belittling
Agenda on which
We have been placed.
We cannot allow
An X to be placed
On our children
Because we know that
They can be made into
A generation of hope
And promise and rejuvenation.
We cannot mess up
The foundation that
Has been laid for us
By failing to request the recognition
Of the richness and beauty
Of our heritage.
In this age,
We cannot duplicate
The standards of the world at large,
Instead we must send a message
In this mess-age…
WE ARE A PROUD PEOPLE!

Self-Description

absolutely imperfect

perfectly flawed

flawlessly organized

still searching for who

i think I ought to be

constantly changing

reinventing myself all the time

occasionally selfish

great giver of comfort

brilliantly creative

unwaveringly loyal

God-fearing

searching for peace

great giver of love

Stolen Innocence

He stole from her
A simple innocence
That can never be returned.

Without permission
From anyone and
Without remorse for
His action,
He shattered her
From the inside out.

Coupled with fear
And an inability to comprehend
This brutality,
The offense has been
Embedded in her young mind.

She has continued to
Ask God "why?"
Though it has been 20 years since,
She has gone on a continual quest
to persevere.
To eradicate tragedy with triumph,
To supplant pain with joy,
To supersede hurt with pleasure,
To usurp fear with faith,
To preempt distrust with trust,
To displace nervousness with self-assurance,
To substitute trepidation with fortitude,
To replace discomposure with boldness.

And in time,
As she continues to seek the face of God,
She now feels the hand of God.
As God decorates her face with time,
And fills her life with understanding,
She will hold tight to the peace of God
As He shines grace and deliverance her way
By allowing her to live without allowing
The past to confine her.

Barack Obama

He stands before
Audiences of thousands—
A brown-skinned symbol
Of hope and change.

The words glide
Slowly from his mouth
Carefully chosen,
Spouting a vision
Of Martin Luther King, Jr.
Inspired unity.

Peered upon by those
Who question the timing
Of this labeled revolution
For the new Negro,
The new American people,
The elderly, the generations of new citizens,
The rainbow
Of people that now
Represent our country.
Some simply call it…
Progress.

Though not long in politics,
He gained notoriety
Like a speedway race
Receiving the endorsements
That surprised many.

Michelle by his side,
Daughters at his knee,
Prepared to fight for
His American right
To lead—
Regardless of race, color or creed.

Our Place

(Montsho Books, etc. was the first and only store for,
by and about blacks in the Orlando area.
It opened in 1990 and closed in 2005;
Founded by Melva "Jackie" Perkins.
Dedicated in loving memory of James R. Smith, II)

Our place was filled with
History and information
About our culture
And our dreams
And our achievements.

The walls were adorned with
Pictures of brown-skinned faces
Who have contributed
So much to our heritage.

With colorful covers
Of books that bespoke
Our lives, our ways, our people—
The shelves brought delight
To the eyes.

The spirit was almost
Symphonic,
You could hear the tribes of Africa
In the background.

And we called it 'Montsho',
Which means "black" in a language
In Botswana.

It was founded by an educator
Whose passion was reading.
Instead of creating an oasis just for her students,

She decided to create an entire
world where people could read
and fall in love with books
over and over again!

Oh we lived there,
We loved there,
We held book signings there,
Fellowship meetings there
Birthday celebrations there,
Story times there,
Festivals there,
Live broadcasts there,
And Tom Joyner stopped by
And left his imprint there.
We represented the new Negro—
The culture behind us,
In front of us,
And the one developing in between.

We held "Jambo Means Hello"
And it was a success.
As people from all around
Came to hear and see,
The great storyteller Dorothy Johnson,
Who presented so lively and boldly!
They poured in by crowds and learned so
Much during this time, it's when many
Developed a place for Montsho permanently
In their hearts and minds.
Gwendolyn Brooks, Rosalyn McMillan,
Tananarive Due, Victoria Christopher Murray,
Lolita Files, Eric Jerome Dickey,
And Anita Bunkley came by.
E. Lynn Harris was there,
And when the literary divas came to town,
Montsho was the host family,

And even off-site we shared
The literature of the very living
Nikki Giovanni, Maya Angelou, Ashley Bryan
Debrena Jackson Gandy, Faith Ringgold and bell hooks
And those gone home to glory
Like Zora Neale Hurston, Nella Larson,
And Daryl Dance.

Oh they came and signed books,
And they gathered for chats,
Jessie and Evelyn McGee Stone
Performed their live music,
And others told stories
From the motherland.

And Frank Frazier came by
And showed off his art
And all kinds of people came by
To see this craft.
We featured the beauty of our people,
Our blackness with
Books by and for our people,
There was Gloria Naylor, J. California Cooper,
James Baldwin, Langston Hughes
And so many more.

Our manager was a great Morehouse man,
Jimmie II was his name,
Finding books to match anyone's preference
Was his special gift from God.
He knew the shelves like
The back of his hands,
Had read every book (some twice)
And in his heart and mind
Were the stories,
The titles, the riddles,
He would recite,

To help to find
The reader's best fit.

Sometimes the people came
From around the world
To this location,
To see the constant great sensations.

But we learned more than just
words and stories there,
We built families, and dreams
And planted seeds
For people who might have
Been trying to find their way.

At Montsho,
They were inspired,
They got more than
That for which they came,
They knew us all
By face and even by name.

We were the community
At large,
The family on the corner there.
And we made our mark for over 15 years
That allowed a venue for
Our people to come and share.

Making A Difference

(For Melva "Jackie" Perkins)

Understanding our roots
Is important for our
Own edification.

Knowing of our struggle
Is significant in its occurrence.
We need to continually
Knock down these barriers
With anticipation for
A brighter tomorrow.

We must be cognizant
Of the strength of
Our brave ancestors,
So that we can draw from it.
Our lives are inspiration
For the next generation.
Our mistakes, misfortunes,
Regrets and reforms are tools
For making a change.

Our successors and accomplishments
Tell of the struggles they've faced
So that we may
Not have to travel
As difficult a path,
For we have borne the burdens
Of our children.

Our voices are powerful
Mechanisms of reinforcements.
We are the inspiration
For making a difference.

We are responsible for
Nurturing the thoughts
Of our young children,
Their thoughts,
Their futures—
It is up to us
To help young people to
Make a difference in this world.

You Are

(For Rebecca Faye Spencer Butler)

You are beautiful and full of beauty.

You are a treasure that has been too long buried.

You are a flower that is in need of a little sunlight,
some tender love and care to fully blossom and grow.

You are a star that has been hidden by bad weather,
but it's going to clear up and your shimmer
will be picture perfect.

You are a special blessing, precious and dear.

Baby Boy

He could have been anything
He set his mind to be
Had he known that he had
A mind that was full of wonder
And possibility,
But he never had a chance
To see another side
Of the world
And before he knew it,
He was thinking about when
He'd start standing on the corner
Like his older brother and father had done.

Although his academics were in tact
And colleges were sending him letters
To invite him to come to
Their schools to play ball
And get an education
FOR FREE,
As long as he did one for the other,
And still, he didn't pay it any attention,
For he really didn't think he could
Do what those college people
Were asking him to do.

His brother had made All-American
And won every award there was to win
And still he'd gone to the corner,
Stayed on the corner and did well
For himself,
Well by the streets' standards,
And he wore his corner status like a cloak
And from one day to the next
He feared for his life

Not knowing if the next car pulling up would
Be an undercover officer or
Someone from another turf,
But brother never shared his fear
And so Baby Boy went on
Thinking that this was the life he wanted to live.

And months went by before
His senior year would end
And coaches kept calling
While his own coach continued to encourage
Him to try new territory
And Brother, still on the corner,
Heard about this chance
And finally told
His little brother
To seek more than he'd seen,
To grow in a way that the streets
Could not teach him,
To find, for the first time,
In generations of their lives,
The courage to move forward,
To do as no one had done,
To break the cycle
And to trust that God would
Give Him the strength
To leave Mama, Grandmamma
And even him behind.
Brother finally told him
The fear he lived with daily—
How he slept in his fabulous house
With his finger on the trigger
Of a gun under his pillow,
How every sound at night made him
Jump with fear,

And that his life was not glamorous
And the streets had not been his friend
And the pain had been too great to comprehend.
Baby boy got the message.
He graduated and left for summer school
And finished his first year with high honors,
Majored in Biology and played his sport well.
Baby boy came home
To bury his big brother,
Who had been killed on that same corner
Gunned down, assassinated.
But big brother had left Baby Boy a message
In a note he had written just
Days before his death.
The note said,
"Dear Baby Boy:
You are everything I ever wanted to be,
Be strong! Love, Brother"

And Baby Boy
Read the note
Given to him by his mother,
And he cried and cried and cried
Some more and when he came
To himself he realized
That he had to succeed,
In order to make a difference
For generations to come.

Unbroken

Your entire life has been inconspicuous.
Your movements,
Your interests,
Your brilliance,
Your gifts,
Your existence,
Your relationships or lack thereof,
Are cold reminders of
Your self-selected solitude.

You have become prisoner
To the wall—
It surrounds you,
Engulfs you,
Claims you as its own.

Though its erection was
All that you knew to do
At the time.
To protect yourself
From the pain of childhood,
It was behind that wall
That you nestled
And felt some remnants of peace.
Void of voices,
And attachments,
And hugs,
And kisses
And love.
Therefore, when affection did not
Come to you as it should
You were already repelled by it.
And now you do not
Know how to receive it,

Some many years later.
Though the wall was
Created as a safety mechanism,
You have not chipped away
At its pieces.
Instead you have piled on
Bricks and mortar
And elevated its height.
It has kept you from
Doing so many things
And being so many things
And loving so many things.
It has manipulated you into
Believing that you
like the protection it gives,
But it is only a mirage.

It has caused you to
Be barren
In kinships,
In spousal commitments,
In friendships,
In relationship after relationship.

It has kept you from opening yourself
Up to those who seek to
Develop ties with you.
You will not let them bind you,
For you will cut each thread
That you believe is weaved,
Piece by piece,
Strategically.

Sometimes on purpose
And sometimes without even knowing it—
You choke the life
Out of what is growing around you

So that it will not flourish in your heart,
So that it will not connect to you,
So that it will reject you and
You will reject it.
You are so insistent in this construction
That you sabotage it,
Pushing it away so that
The real you can never be revealed.

It's unbreakable, like the concrete
From whence it came.
It is the basis of your purposed superficiality,
And it leaves you with many regrets
That in years to come,
You will see
Were irreplaceable opportunities
To love and to be loved.

If I Had Known My Father Well

If I had been given the opportunity
To know my father well,
I would've begged him
To teach me the outs and ends
Of handling the opposite sex.
My goal would have been to be
On top of it all instead
Of being coerced and confused
Into making bad judgment calls.

If I had been given the opportunity
To know my father's style,
I may have been more graceful,
More compassionate, more kind,
More subdued, more mild.

If I had seen my father's face
Maybe just a time or two
I might have recognized the
Unconnected face
That stares back at me from
The bathroom mirror.

If he just could have said
"Hey Baby Girl"
Or perhaps if he would
Have read me a bedtime story,
I might have been a different
Kind of child—
One with a boldness and not a frown,
And the darkness would not
Have made me fearful

Of what might be after me.
If I had known my father—
Just to see his attitude—
I may have been influenced to
Be more calm, more in tune.

But since my dad was AWOL,
That's absent without leave,
I developed my own character,
I became my own best friend.
I didn't follow his model,
For I have been faithful and true
I view my children as gifts
And they know that as a fact.
Without a doubt in their minds
No matter what the occasion or the time,
Mom will always be PWLK,
That's Present with Love and Kisses.
And to them,
My blooming girl and boy,
I will create
My own legacy to pass on
With the deepest of love.

The Chosen Ones

(Written in honor of Clara Fenderson and the late Joe Fenderson)

Age is not a number,
It is merely a state of mind.
In life,
Age is only a sign
And measure of wisdom.

Age is merely
A track record
For God's record
Book of life.
The aged are
The Creators,
The Innovators
Of the progress
That has been
Made to date.

Be proud of your number,
For you are…
The Chosen Ones.

The Ties That Bind

Kaleidoscope

The bond begins, some say in
Intricate transmittals within
The womb…right from conception.
Some say the connection
Is created over time
After nursing nutrients have been exchanged,
When injuries are pampered,
Sicknesses are doctored upon,
And late night storytelling and cuddling
Have taken their proper place.

Its solidarity can move mountains
Or shake a foundation in volcanic eruption.
The connection has come undone
When it has been softened by hurt,
Crushed with disappointment
Befuddled by confusion,
Shattered by rejection and rebuttal,
Riddled with trials, disenchantments and
A failure to thrive.

When the bond dissipates from its oceanic status,
It slowly drains into a lake
And into a pool
Until finally it becomes a puddle
Ready to simply be soaked up by the sun.

The dissipation of this bond has led many daughters astray—
Astray to streets, and to people and to things
That by anyone's account is a tragic link
To the goodness in them.

Lives of young women
Have been impacted, halted, ruined and taken,
Brutally and tragically

As they search for the love that
Their mothers and grandmothers
Gave them sometimes until it hurt,
Tried to give them,
Could not give them,
Did not know how to give
Or was not capable of giving.

Young women who were born of mothers,
Still searching for themselves,
Who became mothers well before their time,
Ill-equipped, ill-prepared and unaware
Of what it meant to give life
And what it meant to give love.
Still, they mourn the loss of daughters gone astray.

And young women born to mothers
Who waited in prayer
And supplication before the Lord,
To give life
Fully prepared and engaged to
Nurture and protect,
Defend and honor,
Teach and learn as well,
Compassionately and passionately loved their daughters,
Without regret, without thought or consideration.
These mothers did love—
They loved as their mothers had loved,
Loved intently and without
Regard for themselves and sometimes
Their own dreams were deferred.
They, too, mourn the loss of daughters gone astray.
For the world calls daughters,
Calls them loudly and by name.
The world's slickness calls them and tells them

The very thing that they want to hear.
And says "I love you"
When they need to hear it most.
And out of desperation, daughters flee,
Flee right to the world
To find what they believe is
The love that they feel is absent from their lives
Daughters look for it…
In men,
In clubs and parties,
In substances,
In relationship after relationship,
In friends,
In jobs and careers,
In people,
In THINGS.

And finally, some daughters,
Some woe-be-gone daughter,
Some born-again-taught-right-and-knew-better daughter,
Some didn't-know-any-better-and-did-the-best-she-could-do
daughter,
Some rebellion-filled-now-revived daughter,
Some once wayward daughter,
Some daughters,
Who managed to survive the world,
Come home.

Hope for Tomorrow

(For my grandfather, Albert Patrick,
who has always given me hope.)

Look, if you will,
Into the eyes of the free.
Learn from my hands,
Rough and torn.
Feel my pain
From the labor
I've borne.
I was born to be
A survivor.

See my spirit,
Vivacious and proud.
Observe my voice,
Loud and strong.
Know of the struggle
That I went through for you
So that you could be born
A survivor too.

Look on these things
As a precious part
Of your history.
Stand up with
Your chest out,
Your hands by your
Side and shout,
"I AM THE HOPE FOR TOMORROW!"

Grandfathers

(For Albert Patrick, Isaac E. Williams and Royce Williams)

Grandfathers are sweet gentle kisses
When you've fallen and bumped your knee.

Grandfathers pour milk into
The sugary bowl of cereal
That Momma and Daddy
Don't want you to eat.

Grandfathers are partners
On front porch swings,
Enjoying the cool
Of a summer sunset and breeze.

Grandfathers are sideline cheerleaders
When victories are plentiful or few.

Grandfathers are pep-talk givers
When triumphs don't come through.

Grandfathers are love and happiness
When the blues
Of a broken heart overcomes you.
Grandfathers are the voice of reason
When you don't know what to do.

Grandfathers are how you know
That God can be everywhere
And anywhere at the same time.

Grandmothers

*(In loving memory of Pearl Bell, Gussie Mae Bright,
Mary Herriott, Roslyn Jones, Julia Patrick Jones, Ruth Nix,
Alberta Johnson Patrick and Muriel Watkins)*

Grandmothers are morning hugs
With a tender squeeze,
Goodbyes from weekend visits
Filled with memories
Of baking chocolate chip
And sugar cookies
With colorful sprinkles on top.

Grandmothers are the carriers
Of ointment and bandages
For scraped knees
From falling off of bicycles
And things,
And the makers of the best
Ham sandwiches with the
Sweetest grape flavored kool-aid
On the side to wash them down.

Grandmothers are the glue
That holds the family together
When tragedies occur
And triumphs are celebrated.

Grandmothers are the initiators
when interventions are needed
When rebellious children
Have lost their way,
Or when habits have developed
That affect the family…
Grandmothers step in to
Institute an improved change.

Grandmothers are genuine love and care,
Hugs and gentle kisses,
Band-aids on bruised knees
And picnics under the trees
And all of the niceties in between.

Grandmothers were created by God
To let us know that adults can
Have compassion and love for us…
Especially when we are much smaller
Than they are and have no voice
To be heard of our own.

Mothers

Mothers are good morning kisses
And hot breakfast fixers,
Gentle correctors with love
And sometimes regret entangled in their voices.
Mothers are loving hugs
And injury menders,
But what they are not good at
Is being a pretender.

Mothers are bedtime storytellers
And midnight prayer warriors.
When difficulties arise
And no one can surmise
What the outcome will be,
Mothers get down on their knees.

Mothers are hand holding partners
And refreshing drink givers,
And they alone are the laundromat
Where our clothes are constantly
Washed and folded and patched.

Mothers are underpaid and underrated,
Underappreciated and undercompensated,
Sacrifice makers and love givers
Who sometimes speak not a word
Of what they need.

Family

through thick and thin

sunshine or rain

for sentimental reasons

in celebrations

of all kinds

standing, anticipating, waiting

to applaud

the occasion

to share in joy

or dry the tears

enjoying the memories

created for the days of tomorrow

stitching pieces into

the fabric of our lives

Tribute To Mom

(For my mother, Maude Johnson Walker)

I am thankful for your love.

I am grateful for your care.

I am delivered by your thoughfulness.

I am refreshed by your view.

I am delighted by your smile.

I am empowered by your support.

I am, who I am today,

Because of the many gifts you've given me,

And the most precious of those gifts...life.

Sisters-in-Law

(For Shenekia Williams-Johnson & Sheneaise Williams)

It has never mattered what chapter

Of our lives had begun.

It has never mattered what state we

Were in, physically or mentally.

It has never mattered what our

Opinions were or the level to which

We approved…

We never considered anything

When it came to loving

Our families,

Bringing them together

On one accord,

Building the foundation

And binding the ties of our children,

nieces and nephews

To us and to those around us.

It has never mattered the time nor the season,

For we know,

Based on example,

The desires that we have

To continue with a legacy

Of love

For our family

And for one another.

My Granddaddy

(For Albert Patrick)

I brag at the confidence

That assures me of your

Well-earned status

High above the clouds—

On the pedestal where I've placed you

From birth and as long as I can remember,

You have been my stabilizer,

My rock, my sustainer,

Holding me above water,

And keeping me from drowning—

Never allowing me to sink

To the bottom.

Your love, like time,

Is guaranteed to come.

You are my one sure thing!

A Connection of the Heart

(For Tammy Wilson Bright, Leslie "Nikki" Bright, Tameka Mitchell Baker, Annette Bright, Kenya Lovell, Alicia Bright Monroe, Lakiesa Bryant Boykin, Tiffany Hines and Natasha Hines)

Though we are connected by

The vows to our mutual loved ones,

We have found in one another

The compression of togetherness

Through trials and tribulations,

Through childbirths and birthdays,

Through graduations and sports venues,

And baby blessings and celebrations of many kinds

And even funerals.

We have held one another by the hand

To show our love.

We have prayed with one another

To solidify our strength.

We have cried with one another

To share our pain.

We have preached to one another

To show our concern.

We have cheered for one another

To show our support.

We have embraced one another

To show our compassion.

And through every season of our lives

We are there,

To lean on each other,

To uplift each other,

To teach each other,

To learn from each other,

To help one another,

To lead one another

And sometimes to follow one another.

Our connection is legal by documentation,

But we are connected at the heart…

By choice.

My Sistergirls

(For Tito Jovan Benjamin, Hope Bryant, Victoria Harris Fitzgerald, Shalott Hazzard, Stephanie Humose, Mariel Jordan Hutchins, Monica Jenkins, Carmen Jones, Alicia Latimore, Anita McMurren, Monica Council Murray, Ashley Joi Oldham, Chelsea Pickens, Camille Hoze Sears, Tamara Taylor, Tracy Taylor, Tammy Thurman, Diane White, Manda & Michelle Wright)

In times of sorrow
When tears are flowing down your cheeks
At the graveside of a child
At the funeral of a grandmother
At a divorce hearing
In the midst of a custody battle
At the bedside of a father
When the pain never seems to cease
And the dark nights never
Seem to come to an end…
I will be there to lift you up.

On days when
Happiness overwhelms you,
When engagements are proposed,
Announced, or if sadness invades
When they are reconsidered or terminated,
When life and spirit may
Be listless or bountiful,
I will be there to share in
Both joy and sadness…
I will lift you up.

When wedding gowns are chosen
And parties are being planned
When your son/daughter is in a play
And is too little for us to understand
What exactly he/she is trying to say…
I'll be there anyway.

When labor pains begin
And reality sets in,
And you and hubby need a few days
Away from the hustle and bustle of life,
I'll rearrange my calendar,
Make time to fill in while you're gone
Because Sistergirls take care of one another that way!

When things go wrong—
Because you know sometimes they will,
When fear overcomes
And your thoughts are unclear
When these doubts come about,
Even if you scream and shout,
I'll be right there to cover my ears.

When an issue arose, like back in the day—
Even back in high school
And our college years,
We've stayed in the fight—
Never leaving the rink,
Getting bumps and bruises
Sometimes 'til we turned pink,
Fought the good fight
Encouraged each other
All along the way
Held one another by the hand
Shed some tears
Fought on occasion

But never a day did we
Not come together
To show our love
As Sistergirls.

Though we don't talk regularly
And sometimes not for years,
We are always on the scene
When we know there are
Needs to be filled.
So if you forget,
The promises we made,
Think of the times
We've cleaned the slate
Picking up just like we left off
And loving like we've always loved...
Remember Sistergirl,
When times get rough...
I will lift you up
Just as you have
Always lifted me!

Motherfriends

(For all those who've reached out to a young girl in need of direction)

A motherfriend is one who
God allows to come into
The life of a young girl who is in
Need of guidance, instruction and love.

A motherfriend may give advice
And even when her adopted daughter
Does the contrary,
She still says "I love you."
And when daughters have been wronged,
Though they know the source of her pain,
She would never say "I told you so."
For a motherfriend holds the secrets
Of a young girl's true self
And loves her just the same.

A Motherfriend shares both laughter and tears,
To help console in a season of difficulty,
Just as if she'd spent hours in childbirth with the daughter.
A Motherfriend feeds her when she's hungry,
Scolds her when she is wrong
And advises her when she is stubborn.

A Motherfriend speaks and says
"Faith is the substance of things hoped for"
Even if her young daughter replies
"I hope for more than faith."

A Motherfriend is a woman to
Whom a young woman will reveal her whole heart
Without ever feeling vulnerable
And even with it in her possession,
A motherfriend will never divulge it to a soul.

A Motherfriend will lay her heart
On the line to and with her daughter,
And even when the daughter's failures
Break the Motherfriend,
She asks for no redemption,
She simply continues to love.

A motherfriend teaches
The capacity to love.
She teaches by example what it
Means when God says
That the older women
Are to teach the younger women.

It is the heart of a motherfriend
That has saved the life of many young girls
Who may not have been able to
Connect with their own mothers,
May not have had a mother,
May not have listened to their mother,
Or may not have known that she wanted to be mothered.
A Motherfriend is God's gift to a young woman in need.

Motherfriends are all types of women.
Some have given birth many times,
While some have never given birth at all.
For God created mothers,
Just as he created friends—
As a direct reflection of His love.

Friendship

(For Delores A. Rush)

Laughter until there are tears

Conversations that seem to go on for years

Advice that comes from the voice of experience

Helping me to overcome my fears

Trust that needs not be requested

Hope that includes every dream

Loyalty, automatic

Love that gives and gives and gives

Mother, aunt, sister, friend

No titles necessary

Never will it end

Bonded from the day our hearts joined

Instant connection for every season to come

Good Men

(For Marvin W. Allen, I., Birto Benjamin, Sr., Alfred Dunn, Joe Edwards, Henry Ezell, Robert Forté, Louis Hoze, Bishop Tim Jackson, Marvin Johnson, Sr., Bruce McMurren, Bishop Henry Rodmon, Comer Taylor, Derrick Williams, Sr., Freddie Williams and James W. Wilson)

Good men are still…
Faithful servants to God
Diligently seeking wisdom
In leadership roles that are indicative
Of education and commitment to progress
Talented and educated
Giving back to the community,
Remembering it as the fabric of life
Never forgetting from whence they came.

Good men are still…
Passing on wisdom to their children
To continue excellence
Reminding them that it is okay
To fail, but that it is never okay
To give up on trying.

Good men are still…
Loving and devoted to their wives
Treating them as the precious jewels they are
Honoring them as they honor God
With the way in which
They live their lives for HIM
Rare commodities of their kind.

Good men are still…
Warriors for their families
Men, defined by their actions
Not by statistics or preconceived notions
The world really does have…
Good men!

Celebration of Life

Until We Meet Again

I sat by the phone
Waiting on the news
That your release from life support
Had turned out exactly the way that we wanted it to,
But instead, the voice I heard
Sounded as though tears had been plentiful,
And it spoke the words that you were "gone,"
And for just a moment
I wanted to tell the voice to take it back
And tell me something good.

I hung up the phone
And fell to my knees,
Asking God to please help me
To know and understand His will
For your life and why He'd taken you from me.

That night He allowed me to see you again
In my dreams,
And it was as though you were standing right over me,
Telling me to be a "big girl" and to remember
That you are in a better place
With streets of gold,
With a new body that would allow you
To feel no more pain
With a new heart
That would allow you to feel no more
Hurt and disappointment.

And in that state of slumber,
I felt a tear roll down my cheek
For though no one loved you like the Father,
I believe I was next in line,
And your absence made my world seem bleak.

Today I am not the 'little girl' you knew.
I've made some changes along the way.
I never conquered the pots and pans,
As I know you wished I would.
I did the things you'd want me to
And some that might have made you mad,
But I took the lessons that you taught me
And planted a seed of love,
That grows in my heart more and more
As I think of our beautiful time together
On this earth,
And as I look forward to our time together
In God's great Heaven…
Until we meet again!

We Will Not Forget

(In loving memory of Trudie Mae Williams Battle)

Your smile will always be remembered.
You brought happiness to so many people.
Your kindness will never be forgotten,
You touched so many lives.

Your passion for helping others
Is forever etched in our memories.
We hear the angels
Singing praises of thanks to you
In Heaven.

Your love for all of us will be
Continuously honored.
We pledge to love one another
And to love others in your absence.

Your spirit is an heirloom—
You passed it on to all of us.

Your love is contagious—
For it has brought many of us together.

Your life was a testimony—
It will stand as both a tool of learning
And as an example.

Your memory is with us always.
We shall forever cherish it.
And we know that you are watching
Us from above
Still loving and caring for us
As you always did.

We will NOT forget
Who you were to us
And who you taught us to be,
For truly God allowed your
Presence in our lives
To mold us and shape us
To prepare us for our destinies.

You Are Missed

*(For Lucille Abercrombie, Smith Counts, Sr., Gloria Allen Dunn,
O.C. Frazier, Louise Counts Griffin, Ira George Hudgins,
Alzada Jackson, Eliza Kirby, Annie Leakes, Juanita McClendon,
Henry McDaniel, Nellie Miller & Cynthia Williams)*

Your time here,
Though measured by days,
Left a great monument to the world—
And to this place, this society, this community.

You touched hearts,
You gave life through enlightenment—
Sometimes orating history,
Praying the scriptures,
Baking and sewing and mending and loving.
You helped to save souls
And led many to Christ,
You changed lives
By teaching
By preaching
By praying
By counseling
By listening
By mothering and fathering,
By being a friend
A confidant
A provider
A supporter
And a cheerleader.
Your spirit was always
Turning strife to sorrow.

We mourn your deaths,
We miss you greatly,
But we thank God for your presence
In this place, this society, this community.

On this day,
And on many other days,
In our selfishness,
We miss your presence,
We search for understanding,
Realizing that your absence
Means that you are in a better place than we,
And this is all a part of God's plan.

As you look down on us from Heaven,
We feel the warmth of you sending us your love,
That we may hold onto it for a while.
We know that you are
Teaching up there,
Preaching up there,
Reading and spouting history up there,
Counseling up there,
Parenting up there,
Listening up there,
Singing up there
And loving up there.

Until we join you again
And as you sing "Hallelujah" and
"By and by when the morning comes,"
We will dry the tears from our eyes
And smile about our time together and wait
For God's plan to unfold.

Divine Intervention

(In loving memory of Trudie Mae Williams Battle)

Each day I thank God
For blessing me with you.
Each night I kneel and tell Him
How much I miss you.
Although our time was short,
I have no doubt that it was
His divine intervention
From the very start
Of our relationship.

And that each lesson
That you taught me,
Every meal we cooked,
Every brownie we baked,
Every cookie we sprinkled,
Every adventure we took,
Every hour we spent on the telephone,
Every song we sang and knew,
Every gift we gave each other,
Every time you lifted my spirits
Or I lifted yours when you were blue,
Every warm hearted hug you gave,
Every dream you helped me fulfill,
Every heartache we endured,
Every memory we made,
Every tear we shed,
Was all because of
God's divine intervention
And His creation of You!

Daughter Of A King

(For Yolanda Denise King
November 17, 1955 – May 15, 2007)

Some did not recognize her—

May not have known her name.

Her goals in life

Were not predicated on gaining world fame

Meek in spirit

Working for the cause—

Her father's legacy

With her siblings she carried on.

An actress by profession

A lady without argument

Gracefully she encouraged

The lives of those she met.

Speaking to audiences across the nation

Encouraged young people to dare to dream—

Elegant in her example

Martin and Coretta's offspring.

In her absence we ask, "why?"

Remembering with honor

The contributions she made

And how she was able

To positively influence things.

We'll remember her fondly,

For she was the daughter of a King.

Freedom's Price

*(For Ian Weikel October 7, 1974- April 18, 2006
Captain, U.S. Army, killed in Balad, Iraq)*

In Iraq
We lost you
Never to be the same again
Bullets, explosions, terrorists
Taking lives
From mothers, fathers, wives,
And children.

War is painful
Hard to comprehend
Not sure our hearts
Will ever mend.

Tears will fall
Memories replay
We never thought
We'd loose you this way
Fighting for freedom
The high price you've been forced to pay
We hope we'll see you
Again one day.

The Final Goodbye

Last glance as the top is closed

Rolling out of the church

Tears flow as it is lifted into the hearse

At the grave the casket is lowered

Into a heaping mound of dirt

That covers its shine

Goodbye to our loved one

Gone forever

Ascended up to God

For safekeeping

Mistaken Identity

(In loving memory of Jason Rashad Trier)

Before the message became reality

We heard that there had been an accident

Placed the information in reserve

Until it became the truth

Accident, uncomforting

Your presence meant more than words

Your life was headed in the direction of greatness

Humility, kindness, purity, love

We believed that it had to be the wrong person

Perhaps the death angel got things mixed up

This mistaken identity had to be so

Took you before your time was up

Sitting in memorial we feel choked

Our lives had been thrown a horrible blow

We know your spirit is always near

And you'll always know

That you were loved, admired, endeared, adored

And if you'd had just a little more time

We would have seen you do so much more

We'll see you when the times arrives

For now, we'll hold your memory close

And we'll be thankful for the precious time

That we did have…together.

Tributes to the Life
Of
May Lois Bright McCray

Featuring Contributions by:
Gwen B. Baker
Schadre Dent
Ophelia Bright Hines
Tiffany Hines
Chenise Lytrelle
K. Lovell
N. Renée
Imani Williams

Ode To Granny

We learned as much as we could from you

Before you passed away.

But we know that your love

Will forever stay.

I know how many

Lives you have changed.

And, oh yeah,

So many victories you have won.

But the one thing that is for sure:

Your legacy will live on forevermore.

By Imani Williams
(Eldest grandchild of May Lois Bright McCray)

Still We Praise God

We are broken
By your tragic removal
From our lives.
Our words form with
Quivered lips and
Our minds remain heavy
With the weight of
Inexplicable pain.

We ask God to show us
Some mercy,
Some grace,
Some love,
Some explanation,
Some reasoning,
Some understanding,
That might soothe us,
For just a little while.

And although we know that
We are forbidden
To question Him,
And that you would not
Have wanted us to,
We are still struggling
To understand,
To hear His voice in the midst
Of all of this pain,
To function,
To maintain our composure,
To exist,
And sometimes to breathe.

Yet, still we praise God!
We praise Him for
Who you were to us
And who you will always be.
Because of what you've taught us,
We know that God
Is a sustainer!
And we will hold on
To the comfort that
We will find in Him
And in each other,
As we struggle
To accept His will and
This "act of God"
That has been listed
As the cause that
Snatched you from us.

In time we will hold
On to the memories
That we've shared
Over the years.
We will live for those who love us,
We will honor you in
And with our lives,
We will love one another
Through every season,
And we will remember you
As mama, granny, sister, auntie,
Cousin, Pastor, community worker,
Peacemaker and friend.

And as the sun
Sets on the days that pass,
We will keep your legacy alive by
Continuing to be
The kind of God-fearing people
That God will allow
To enter the gates,
So that we can see you again,
And still we will praise God…
Together again!

By Chenise Lytrelle
(Daughter-in-law of May Lois Bright McCray)

Don't Forget How Much I Love You

Sometimes sisters don't make their feelings clear—
they assume that sisters know
of the deep love
they feel for one another.

Yet, when misunderstandings occur
and things are left unsaid,
Misunderstandings can lead to
needless doubt and insecurities.

I don't want you to feel insecure,
and I want you to remember
these words I am telling you now
because they will always be
current and never changing…
"I LOVE YOU!"

By Gwen B. Baker
(Sister of May Lois Bright McCray)

Time

An irreplaceable entity

Never sufficient

For the little things

Our history

Our Future

Life

And Death

Cause and solution

Of social conflict

Humanly diminutive

Spiritually eternal

By N. Renée
(Niece of May Lois Bright McCray)

Storm

You know I'm on the way home,

Traveling all around the storm.

Yet, I'm pressing my way home.

Valleys great and small, mountains high and low.

Look around headed toward greater towns.

Sometimes weighed to the ground,

Heaven bound and I know it can be found.

Searching round and round.

Too close to be found!

By Ophelia Bright Hines
(Sister of May Lois Bright McCray)

Auntie's Poem

In a minute I'd tell you I love You,
In an hour I'd tell you why,
In a lifetime I'd think of more reasons,
Now all I can do is cry.

It hurts so bad I'm selfish,
I think you should be here with me.
I've had long days, long hours, but
That's still how I think things should be.

So many things in my life are missing,
Like you being here to wipe my eyes,
To tell me it's ok and hold me while I cry.

If pain is weakness then I'm at my end.
If struggle is strength I can lift 20 men.
I won't ask God because I already know,
He took cuz you were ready; it was your time to go.

I'm glad you found rest, in a place you loved most,
I heard you were on your knees with a Bible close.
In the comfort of God struck only by disbelief,
God gave you a task and that task you did complete.

You led with other's cares in mind,
Driven by what you could give and
Not what you could find.

With your work complete,
Mission now accomplished, and
Triumph over a great feat;
Not much was left for you to do,
For in this case, Satan was beat.

Now man says there must be a cause to go,
And what better way to be,
Cause of Death: "ACT OF GOD,"
To the world it seems odd,
The Lord spoke, "Child Rest In Peace!"

By Tiffany Hines
(Niece of May Lois Bright McCray)

Ready or Not

People dyin' all over who ain't never died before
Fallin' off like marbles through a board in a rotten floor.

Mothers and Fathers, He's callin' them all
They got the nerve to answer, as if just going behind a wall.

They leavin' chullen and spouses to mourn their loss —
Families in chaos left to suffer their great loss.

People dyin' all over who ain't never died before —
Young people, old people, bought and sold people.

Now don't you fret and don't hesitate to cry
Feel free to call on Him and just ask "Why?"

Now He will answer but perhaps, not right away,
When He does you be careful and pray.

Don your Rose of Charin, kiss this horrid world goodbye,
Get ready so the beloved Father won't pass you by.

By K. Lovell
(Niece of May Lois Bright McCray)

Losing Someone

Gone,
Away, never to return to this disgusting world
Pain,
Taken away from us,
They gon' be happy in another place.
But it's hard to let go,
I don't want to let go.

Gone,
I can't live without you—
Don't want to live without you.

Pain,
Things were painful when you lived,
But I was going to be here helping you
To make it through.

I don't want to believe that you are gone—
I am not going to let go,
Because if I let go,
Your memories will leave,
The collection of thoughts—
Your words, I remember
Sometimes you spoke them so point blank.

I am losing them,
But I'm not going to let go.
I don't want to let go.
But I have to.
For God's sake,
Why am I
Always losing someone?

By Schadre Dent
(Great Niece of May Lois Bright McCray)

New Voices

Featuring Contributions by:
Briana Allen
Tameka Baker
Schadre Dent
Eugenia F. Forté
N. Renée
Tracy A. Taylor
Evan White
Imani Williams

Why?

Why?

Why do I have to deal with the pain everyday,

The pain of my great-grandmother, uncle

And granny passing away?

Why do I ask this?

It's because of the pain.

The pain is closing in on me

Everyday until I can't breathe?

Gasping, gasping, gasping for air

Until suddenly I have to stare.

I don't know why and I don't care,

So I just stare.

And then hopefully

I see a glimpse

Of the future with

Mommy, Daddy, my brother and me.

By Imani Williams

Questions I Ponder

Is this the tree

Where my brethren hanged?

Or is this the ground where

he was burned?

These are the questions

that I ponder

in my head everyday.

Why did people treat us so badly?

And why right now are people out

fighting a senseless war

When... all we need is world peace?

By Imani Williams

We Are Strong

We are strong!

We are stronger than

a million men put together .

We are women!

We have a history of strength—

Like Rosa Parks and the bus boycott,

or Coretta Scott King's efforts for freedom with her husband,

And, of course, Oprah Winfrey,

for bringing people together

to change the world.

And there are many more!

So remember…

We are strong black women!

By Imani Williams

I Love My Mom

I love my mom
because she is so sweet.
I love her because she is so neat.
Her love is like a wave
that keeps on flowing
and never ever stops.

Whenever I feel
sad or lonely,
her love comforts me,
and when I need a good laugh,
she is always there.

So you see I will always be
a big momma`s girl.
I will love my mommy
from this time and forever more.

By Imani Williams

Poem 1

I always pretend not to have it

I try to avoid it

when I know I need it

Afraid of heart break?

yes

Afraid of deception?

absolutely

I cannot let myself down,

but then

what is it exactly

I say it when I don't mean it

I let others feel it

for me

I break hearts

I deceive

I let others down,

but

why?

By N. Renée

Poem 2

Sometimes I think about

You know, you and me

and what it would be

like if I and you

were we, us, them, or they.

The things that embody

my man,

form you.

As you describe your

ideal woman

I am created.

There are those deep

valleys in my heart

that only you have traveled.

You never cease to amaze me

I adore, respect, concern, and yearn

for you and me, he and she

to be one.

By N. Renée

Poem 3

It's my desire for you

that electrifies my synapses

Entering my thoughts

when I least expect it

Is it all in vain?

Distance separates our bodies,

but our minds seem to connect

Is it realistic?

Do I reverberate in you?

As time passes

my visions of our future

fade

If we are meant

To be,

will we be?

I see me in you, but

do you see you in me?

By N. Renée

Inapt

Arrogant despite his ignorance

he flaunts

Taunting the intelligence

he has failed to achieve

while basking in mediocrity

Blissful knowing nothing,

but convinced he knows all

Self-proclaimed perfection, so

he strives for nothing more

Detrimentally influenced by

those surrounding him

that praise his unsuccess

So confident, in fact,

he dares to reproduce

He possesses unshaken

faith that his methods are optimal

This is regurgitated

to his children

Consequently echoing

in the community

fortifying our ruin

By N. Renée

Inspirable Person

Inspirable person, you fill my world with joy.

Inspirable person, I know you'll never take me for a toy.

Inspirable person, you are a real coach to me.

Inspirable person, you are the water in my sea.

Inspirable person the thing

I want to say to you is I know you see.

I write it across my face,

So you can see it up close or afar.

Inspirable person you teach me things

Just the way they are,

I know you won't let my secrets out of the jar.

Inspirable person, you know who you are,

A teacher,

A coach,

A woman of power,

You will forever be my inspiring person for every hour.

Inspirable person…you are!

By Schadre Dent

Prayer Is The Language Of God

I am saved!
I am a child of God.
I am blessed and highly favored.
I am valued.
I am the head and not the tail.
I am Loved unconditionally by God.
I am anointed.
I am blessed and not cursed.
I am fearfully and wonderfully made.
I am HEALED.
I am gifted.
I am the salt of the earth.
I am HAPPY.
I have a bright future.
I am FORGIVEN...
I am a part of God's Family.
I am a part of a Royal Priesthood.
I am rich and not poor.
I can do all things through Christ who strengthens me.
I am excited by God's love and not mans'
I am BEAUTIFUL.
I am changed...
I have the favor of God.
I am somebody; I'm God's child.
I am grateful and thankful.
I am a daughter/son of God...
I am of a chosen generation...
I am of a holy nation...
I am a citizen of heaven...
I am above and not beneath...
I am a joint-heir with Jesus Christ...
I am the redeemed of the Lord that say so…
I am treasured….
As said in Acts 26:2, I think myself happy…
I am more than a conqueror through Christ Jesus.
And my latter days shall be better than my former days.

By Eugenia F. Forté

My Mother Is Like

(For Charlene Stallworth Allen)

My mother is like a pendulum
At the beginning of the day
Her mood is cheerful, at a high point.

Stress and our demands of her
Cause her mood to eventually swing down
But I know at the end of the day
It will be back up again.

My mother is like the roots of a tree
Strong, quiet, and at times unseen
She continuously supports our family
Whether or not we give her the water she needs
To do so.

My mother is like a queen
Always dressed to impress
Jewelry, heels, and a matching outfit
Hair, never out of place.

I am like my mother
Or at least one day
I would like to be.

By Briana Allen

The Duality of Love

It was a cold, lonely day
My world rested at a stand still
All I knew did not exist anymore
Heartbreak had arrived and consumed me
My thoughts
My happiness
My normal consistency in life
Love seemed so simple
An unexplainable feeling that arrived
Regardless of my will
So I embraced it and
It became my foundation
If I could count on nothing else
Love would see me through
It amazed me
How something so easily attainable
Was so painful and difficult to lose
To give up on
To let go of
Even more surprising was the cure
The anecdote that I found
To heal my broken heart
Was love itself
And though the pieces didn't quite
Fit the same
Slowly, I regained everything back
My thoughts
My happiness
My normal consistency in life

By Briana Allen

Balance...

...is what keeps me from lashing out when
  "wrong doing" is directly in front of me,
  masked as "right."

...is the key to good communication.

...prevents someone else's dysfunction from
  weaving its way into becoming yours.

...helps me love those that are weak
  minded, and threatened by the God-given
  drive I have within me.

...is where I go when everything
  seems uncertain.

...is what I have become for others.

...is God's hand on my shoulder guiding me
  through the course that He set for me & helping
  me gently get back on course when I stray.

By Tracy A. Taylor

Lies

The lies you tell
    break the hearts of others.

The lies you tell
    create new worlds.

DARK WORLDS! FALSE WORLDS!

TRANSPARENT WORLDS!

Because of your lies
    no one trusts you.

NOT EVEN YOU!!!

You destroy molded bonds…

You tarnish polished reputations…

You make the very confident, uneasy…

What's most important to you, is you…

Which is the biggest lie!

By Tracy A. Taylor

God's Sacred Covenant

Standing at the alter
Earthly Representation of the Throne of God
Love that binds two
In the presence of Him
Embarking on a Journey

Growing with each passing year
Life Love Children Family
Words and Thoughts Blending Together
Perfect Harmony
Bearing Fruit

Children
Walking, Breathing Reminders
Ultimate Expression of Love
Perfect Blend of Two
Taking the Best of Each

Unity
Faithfulness
Imperfections
Weaknesses
Strengths
Sharing
Grief
Disappointment
Dreams
Goals
Silent Understanding
Sickness and Health
Braced by the Lord
Spiritual Union

God's Sacred Covenant

By Tameka Baker

Our Generation

Why do we live our lives in such fear
Maybe it's because,
we believe what we hear.

We live each day
trying to prove it's Wrong;
Yet, we live our lives
through TV and negative Song;
Saggin', Thuggin', Robbin' and Killin';
Our Generation declares,
A Generation for Healin'.

If being a player is part of your Dream,
think beyond the court;
Aspire to own an entire team;
Excel in math
and read more than required;
Life's blueprint and become inspired.
As the negative glares begin to cease,
Our Generation can live,
our life in PEACE.

Our ancestors were
Humiliated, Beaten and Lynched,
for Goodness Sake;
Why do we ignore it,
as if it were fake.
When we realize this,
We have no right to complain.
Our possibilities are unlimited
If we'd **E-X-P-A-N-D** our Brain.

We cannot live our life blaming them all;
Our Generation must get to work
and answer God's call.

This message should stay
in the forefront of your mind.
The more we ignore;
the longer we'll remain behind.

We'll ignore the negative
things that are said;
We know true Power;
it's all in our head.
Instead of condemning,
the lives of our youth,
Lead us and teach us
the painful truth.
Redirecting our steps
is first you see;
In order to become,
what **GOD**…wants US 2 BE!

I just stopped by to
plant some seeds in your head,
"DON'T GET IT TWISTED"
Our Generation is not DEAD!

By Evan White

Acknowledgements

As this project has been in its birthing stages, I must thank my family for their undying love, support and patience; I am grateful to my husband, Isaac Abayomi Williams and our wonderful children, Imani and Malik, for being my biggest fans! I love you with all of my heart.

For my lifetime inspiration, I have to thank my grandfather, Albert Patrick, who is my rock and who has always been the one to keep from drowning.

To my mother, Maude Johnson Walker, thanks for the most precious gift that anyone can receive; life! Thank you to my brother, Bakari Worthy (B. Worthy Productions), the budding producer, for his creativity in producing the spoken word version of this project.

I am eternally grateful to my entire family who is always on my side. Abundant thanks to the best father-in-law in the entire world, Isaac E. Williams and to my sisters-in-laws, Shenekia and Sheneaise, who are always a source of support. To all of my (maternal, paternal and in-laws) uncles, aunts, cousins and relatives who are encouragers, you can never know how much it means!

For the efforts of my dear friends, loved ones and confidants who served as readers, editors and critics, I extend my gratitude and my deepest love. Thank you to Jean Bryant, Jolene Ezell, Robert and Eugenia Forté, Dr. Valencia Matthews, Dr. Margie Rauls and Patricia Wilkins. And especially to Delores A. Rush ("Mama Delores") who read through more poems than anyone can ever imagine.

To many of the loved ones, relatives and friends referenced in these pages, thank you for sharing your lives, your stories, your hearts with me over the years. To all those named and unnamed who celebrate and applaud my efforts and projects, thank you from the bottom of my heart! God has a way of sending us angels in the form of people at various intervals! I am thankful for all of those who are a continual source of strength and support for me and my family, many of them are a part of the dedications of these poems and are the inspiration for a number of them.

To my children's godparents and my second family, without whom I wouldn't have been able to accomplish the milestones that I have in the last 17 years; Special thanks to Dr. Tito Benjamin, Birto & Joanne Benjamin and Ceddie Wilson.

Thank you to Rosalyn McMillan for her literary inspiration and advice that emerged into a friendship. To Rev. Dr. Arlene Churn (my godmother and personal spiritual advisor) without whose encouragement this collection would never have been born. Thank you for the opportunity that you provided for me to share my work with the world in your book, *The End Is Just the Beginning: Lessons in Grieving for African Americans* (Random House, 2003).

Thank you to MaryAnn Rifenberry and Heidi Gouge, at the Baker Press who were an integral part of this project and who assisted me in bringing this book to fruition.

About the Author

Chenise Lytrelle is the author of *Life's Lessons*. In 1996, she received a national writing award for her original choreopoem: *The Bare Essentials of Blackness*. Her work also appears in *The End Is Just the Beginning: Lessons in Grieving for African Americans* by Dr. Arlene Churn (Random House, 2003). Chenise is an educator and a motivational speaker. Additionally, she is the founder of the Anointed Publishing Company. She is married to Isaac A. Williams and they have two children, Imani and Isaac Malik. She and her family reside in Springfield, Virginia.

About the Contributors

Briana Allen is a graduate of Glenelg High School in Glenelg, Maryland and is a native of Orlando, Florida. She is the eldest child of Marvin (I) and Charlene Allen. Briana is currently attending Howard University and is majoring in Interior Architecture.

Gwen Bright Baker is a nurse manager with the Veterans Administration Medical Center in Gainesville, Florida. She is a graduate of Florida A&M University and the University of Phoenix. She currently serves as the pastor of Bethel Freewill Baptist Church in Lake City, Florida.

Tameka Baker is a native of Macon, Georgia and a graduate of Florida A& M University. She is currently pursuing a Master's degree in Health Administration. Tameka works as a researcher for The Institute of Faith Health Leadership. She is the wife of Pastor Gregory Baker. The couple has two children, Gregory II and Kennedy. They reside in Atlanta, GA.

Schadre Dent is a junior at Andrew Jackson High School in Jacksonville, Florida. She loves to play basketball and write poetry. Schadre is the daughter of Arthur Dent and Tanya Jordan.

Eugenia F. Forté is a business operations analyst at Lockheed Martin. She is a graduate of Bethune Cookman University, where she earned her degree in Business Administration. She is married to Robert Forté. Eugenia and her husband reside in Orlando, Florida.

Tiffany Hines is a graduate of Bradford High School in Starke, Florida and Santa Fe Community College. She is currently attending the University of Florida majoring in Family, Youth and Community Science.

Ophelia Bright Hines is a graduate of Florida A&M University and Rollins College. She is the co-pastor of Bethel Freewill Baptist Church in Lake City, FL. Hines currently resides in Starke, FL and works as a substance abuse counselor.

K. Lovell is the only child of Patricia Lovell and the late Charles Lovell. A graduate of Crescent City High School and Howard University, she is currently pursing her Master's degree in Divinity at Emory University (Candler School of Theology) in Atlanta, GA.

N. Renée is a graduate of Florida State University and Hofstra University. She is also published in the International Library of Poetry anthology and VOX literary journal. N. Renée resides in New York, NY and is a member of Alpha Kappa Alpha Sorority, Inc.

Tracy A. Taylor is a graduate of North Carolina Central University. She currently works as a coordinator for Wake County Human Services. The adoptive parent and long time youth advocate resides in Morrisville, North Carolina.

Evan White is a seventh grade student at The Greenhill School in Dallas, Texas. He enjoys many academic areas including literature, history and art. He is a member of Friendship-West Baptist Church. Evan is the son of Alvin (III) and Diane White.

Imani Williams is a sixth grade honor student attending Newington Forest Elementary in Springfield, Virginia. Her favorite academic subjects include language arts and history. Her hobbies are writing poetry, reading and singing. She is the daughter of Isaac A. and Chenise Lytrelle Williams. She lives with her parents and her younger brother, Malik, in Virginia.

For additional information about

Kaleidoscope: A Collection of Poetry
visit

www.cheniselytrelle.com

The May Lois Bright McCray Memorial Scholarship Fund

A portion of the proceeds from this book will be used to establish The May Lois Bright McCray Memorial Scholarship Fund.

May Lois Bright McCray was the founder and pastor of the Bethel Free Will Baptist Church in Lake City, Florida. She was an educator within the Bradford County School System (Starke, Florida) until her retirement in 2002.

As a pastor and a community worker, Pastor McCray worked diligently to assist young people in reaching their full potential. An advocate for education and progress, she was heralded as an individual who truly believed that "all children can learn."

She was affiliated with the United American Free Will Baptist Church, Inc, Bradford County Democratic Committee, Bradford County Chapter of NAACP (past president) and Zeta Phi Beta Sorority, Inc., to name a few. She was also the founder of Come Together Children Ministries, Inc.

She has left a host of family members to carry out her tremendous legacy. As keepers of the flame of excellence, The May Lois Bright McCray Memorial Scholarship Fund is chaired by her children, Shenekia Williams-Johnson, Isaac A. Williams and Sheneaise M. Williams.